Margaret Feinberg's appetite for the feast of His grace makes you hunger for more of a fulfilling life. Read and taste the richest food for the soul!

SMALL-CAPS ANN VOSKAMP, author of *The Broken Way* and *One Thousand Gifts*

I could not put it down! I lost track of time like reading an adventure novel, when in fact she is writing a factual and biblical documentary. Impressive! I'm the least foodie man on the planet, and yet I loved *Taste and See*.

SHANE FARMER, lead pastor of Cherry Hills Community Church, Denver, CO

Margaret is a storyteller who never ceases to see the beauty of the world around us. If you love God, good food, and life around the table, this book will take you on an unforgettable culinary journey through the Bible.

JENNIE ALLEN, author of *Nothing to Prove* and founder of IF:Gathering

Margaret Feinberg takes us on a gourmet tour of the earth and through the Scriptures that will fill your mind and satisfy your soul. Enjoy this scrumptious read.

KYLE IDLEMAN, pastor and author of *Not a Fan* and *Don't Give Up*

I love Jesus, food, and the Bible . . . not in that particular order, of course . . . if you do, too, then this is the most delicious book you'll read this year!

LISA HARPER, speaker and author of *The Sacrament of Happy*

Feinberg explores the foods of the Bible in this delightful book . . . Christian foodies are in for a real treat.

PUBLISHERS WEEKLY

Only once have I received a prayer request for a friend because she was traveling alone in Israel to master traditional fishing methods and in Croatia to hand-harvest olives. But these escapades typify Margaret Feinberg's research into biblical food—from fish to figs and bread to barbecue—all to nourish us with special spiritual fodder as well as memorable meals. Deliciously written!

CRAIG L. BLOMBERG, Distinguished Professor of New Testament, Denver Seminary

Like an expert chef reaching for only the finest ingredients, Margaret Feinberg seasons her prose with generous dashes of wit and wisdom, whetting our appetites for the bounty of knowledge and inspiration she dishes out, chapter after delicious chapter. Oh, the people she meets and the meals she eats and the places she goes. Inviting us to travel with her from California to Croatia, Texas to Connecticut, Utah to Israel, Margaret reveals how our healthy dependence on food parallels our deeper dependence on the One who provides what our hearts need most. Her writing style is warm, and her message compelling, as she encourages us to taste and see the goodness and richness of God. What a feast!

LIZ CURTIS HIGGS, bestselling author of *Bad Girls of the Bible*

Every Christian I know is looking for what this book provides—HOPE. This book is just like Margaret! Intensely personal, deeply moving, spiritually challenging, and a joy to be around. *Taste and See* is a spiritual goldmine.

RAY JOHNSTON, lead pastor of Bayside Family of Churches

Don't miss this feast from Margaret Feinberg. It's one part rich storytelling, two parts authenticity, and three parts compelling exploration of Scripture. The refreshing images and insights in each chapter of *Taste and See* will nourish your heart and soul. It left me coming back for more.

KARA POWELL, PhD, Executive Director of the Fuller Youth Institute

Margaret takes us on a wonderful, witty adventure to explore the world of food and the Bible. You'll literally travel the globe dining on incredible meals with mesmerizing people, excavating rich spiritual insights, and laughing at the hilarious stories. Make sure you take this journey!

DAVE FERGUSON, lead pastor of Community Christian Church

Taste and See is part cookbook, part Bible study, and part biography. My friend Margaret takes you on an inspiring journey to discover there is more to biblical foods than meets the eye. Believe me—you will love this book.

PHIL WALDREP, founder of Women of Joy Conferences

In this rich and personal book, Margaret invites us to literally *taste* faith, not just believe it. It is an invitation you don't want to refuse. A delectable, grace-filled, God-nurtured world awaits!

NORMAN WIRZBA, Associate Dean at Duke University and author of *Food and Faith*

TASTE
and
SEE

Discovering God Among Butchers,
Bakers & Fresh Food Makers

MARGARET FEINBERG

ZONDERVAN

Taste and See
Copyright © 2019 by Margaret Feinberg

Requests for information should be addressed to:
Zondervan, *3900 Sparks Dr. SE, Grand Rapids, Michigan 49546*

ISBN 978-0-310-35682-0 (audio)

Library of Congress Cataloging-in-Publication Data

Names: Feinberg, Margaret, 1976- author.
Title: Taste and see : discovering God among butchers, bakers, and fresh food makers / Margaret
    Feinberg.
Description: Grand Rapids, MI : Zondervan, [2018] | Includes bibliographical references. |
Identifiers: LCCN 2018036503 (print) | LCCN 2018040618 (ebook) | ISBN 9780310354871 (ebook) |
    ISBN 9780310354864 (softcover)
Subjects: LCSH: Food—Religious aspects—Christianity. | Dinners and dining—Religious
    aspects—Christianity.
Classification: LCC BR115.N87 (ebook) | LCC BR115.N87 F45 2018 (print) | DDC 248—dc23
LC record available at https://lccn.loc.gov/2018036503

Author is represented by The Christopher Ferebee Agency, www.christopherferebee.com.

Cover design: Faceout Studio
Cover photography: Shutterstock / Stocksy
Interior design: Denise Froehlich

First printing November 2018 / Printed in the United States of America

20 21 22 PC/LSCH 10 9 8 7 6 5

To the love of my life, Leif.

*Your strength, courage, wisdom, and grace still take
my breath away. Thank you for picking me.*

To Jonathan and Carolyn.

*Without you two—your love, support, encouragement,
and the "little writing intervention"—this
book would not exist. I love you both!*

Menu

WARNING: The following pages are likely to cause the side effects of becoming spiritually and physically hungry. We recommend devouring the pages with healthy snacks nearby.

An Invitation to a Culinary Adventure

"Let's eat and get out of here as quickly as we can," I whispered to Leif as we unbuckled our seat belts.

My droopy-eyed husband and I were soul-tired from a long, busy season of work, but had previously committed to dinner at a new acquaintance's home. As we pulled into the driveway, I was second-guessing that decision.

Dread grew with each step along the cobblestone path, but there was no backing out now. Leif stopped short at the door and looked at me as if to say, "Go on in, dear. You got us into this." My best hope was to get the evening over with, so I could return to bed and my pajamas. I gripped the door knocker, counted to three, and forcibly transformed my grimace into what I hoped was a believable grin.

The door swung open, and Matthew and Ashley enveloped us in hugs as if we were prodigal children returning home. *Whoosh*—the air around us rearranged, and with it, our attitudes.

Hospitality has a hidden power that is difficult to explain but even harder to deny. You can wake up cranky and sore, but a mere whiff of Mom's holiday sticky buns can bring your shoulders down from around your ear lobes. Or you find yourself drowning in loneliness and, just as tears well in your eyes, the phone rings and a new friend invites you over for a hot beverage and a bowl of fresh berries. One moment the world could burn to dust for all you care, and in a blink, it is sacred ground.

As the German author and poet Christian Morgenstern writes, "Home is not the building you live in; home is wherever you are understood."

Leif and I found home that night—against our wills, no less. These many years later, I still can't explain how it happened. Maybe it was the soothing flicker of candlelight or the broken-in couch that swallowed us whole, but nevertheless, our hearts stilled, and time became irrelevant.

Our more-than-capable host, Matthew, revealed himself as an avid foodie attuned to the finer points of knife-work techniques, the origin of rare ingredients, and the latest culinary breakthroughs. He served us wave upon wave of hors d'oeuvres—jalapeño-stuffed olives, salted pistachios, a charcuterie board of savory meats and exotic cheeses. Each bite tasted better than the last.

An hour after we arrived, Matthew pulled his *pièce de résistance* from the oven—a special-order roast from a local butcher slow-cooked for thirty-six hours. My mouth watered so much I struggled not to slobber on myself, but he informed us the meat needed to rest before we could enjoy. In the meantime, he served us an arugula salad with orange slices and homemade citrus dressing. The meat arrived alongside a fresh Kalamata olive loaf and flash-fried broccoli sprinkled with lemon shavings.

Yep, Leif and I were definitely prodigal children. Every meal prior to this one during our marathon season of work suddenly felt like pig feed. Our hearts weren't brought back to life because the dinner was swanky or exclusive; our hearts revived because the food was intentional and curated with love. The meal nourished my soul in places I didn't realize I was starving.

After dark chocolate ganache flourless cake and specialty roasted coffee, Matthew took us to see an oversized refrigerator in the garage where he cured meat and aged cheeses—the ones we munched on earlier. Then, we followed him to the backyard to see his lush garden boxes of lettuces, an array of spices, and lemon trees.

> The meal nourished my soul in places I didn't realize I was starving.

The four of us talked late into the evening, and I didn't want to leave. By the time we said good-bye, a spiritual bond had formed. We had arrived cranky, sore, and exhausted, but left satiated in our bellies and hearts. Together we had enjoyed the gift of food, the gift of togetherness, the gift of presence. As Christian Morgenstern might say, we came home.

Years later, I recounted the story of that night at another dinner party. To break the ice, the host, Janie, asked the attendees to share about their most memorable meal. When nobody spoke up and the silence became uncomfortable, Janie volunteered to go first.

She described an evening in Venice with her husband. The Italian eatery lacked menus and only had five tables. The chef prepared the meal from fresh ingredients and his latest culinary whim. When the sun-dried tomato focaccia ran out, he sprinted down the street to buy more.

"The mushroom marinara sauce, the romantic setting, the time together, just us . . . that place," she recalls. "The restaurant is gone now and that makes me love it all the more. The memory is frozen in time forever."

Nicholas followed with a memory from his childhood. Growing up in a military family meant bouncing from town to town and base to base. While stationed off the coast of San Diego, his parents slipped him cash for a beachside fish fry.

"I loved the freedom of going alone," he remembered. "I was only ten, and the fish had been caught that day. Moist. Tender. The best filets I've ever eaten."

Next, Emily described a holiday meal surrounded by family and a table laden with pan-roasted turkey, cranberry stuffing, and sweet potato pie: "That was the last Thanksgiving with my grandmother. I still try to follow her recipes, but they never taste as good as when she made them."

After I shared about my remarkable meal with Matthew and Ashley, Yang went last. She described the meal her adopted parents served on the first night she arrived in her new home. They tried to make the transition easier by serving her a syrupy-sweet teriyaki chicken atop mushy Minute Rice.

"I remember wondering how I could live with these people when the food was so bad," Yang said.

We couldn't help but laugh. But then Yang explained that her new mom appeared with dessert. A package of almond cookies from China. They tasted like home, and the tension dissipated.

In exchanging stories about our most memorable meals, we shared more about ourselves than our culinary preferences—we revealed our deeper longings. For Janie, the pasta in Venice uncovered the desire for closeness with her spouse. Nicholas's fish fry revealed his need for independence from a young age. Emily's Thanksgiving memory unveiled the importance of family, tradition, and memories. Yang's almond cookies spoke of a deep need for belonging.

I saw a pattern unfolding before me that I couldn't ignore. The stories were different, but the theme remained the same: God had been intentional in each gathering. He used these encounters to uncover a deep need and satiate a deep hunger.

Driving home, I became curious whether it was all a fluke. Were my friends and I uniquely vulnerable during meal times or were our table experiences shared by others? Was there a connection between spiritual and physical hunger?

I couldn't stop thinking about it. Digging even deeper into my story, I realized that there were layers below the surface of the charcuterie and the thirty-six-hour roast. My deepest hunger was my longing for connectedness and friendship. I was raised by hippie-like parents who moved to new remote locations every few years. Few children ever lived nearby, so I spent much of my youth surrounded by adults and ached for contact with others my age. The few hours I spent with schoolmates in class never felt like enough, and I carried a deep loneliness during childhood. As an adult, I still ache for the rich relationships and the rootedness that comes from knowing and being known. And although my story is unique, I have a suspicion this hunger resides in each of us.

When we exit our mother's womb, the umbilical cord connecting us to our mother is snipped, severing our constant nutritional source, and from that moment on, we are perpetually hungry. Infants hunger for safety and security. Children starve for guidance and knowledge. Adolescents yearn for someone, anyone, to accept them and understand them. Adults crave all manner of things—power and success, recognition and affirmation, belonging and community. At midlife, amid juggling work and family, our longings shift toward questions of impact and influence. In our twilight years, we crave good health, stability, and the grace to finish well.

It's not just our life stages that stoke our deeper appetites. Inherent in every human are longings for meaning and purpose. We yearn to know that God still cares and that the details of our lives really matter. We desire friends who will make us laugh and cry and feel again. We long to be recognized by someone who thinks we're special and smart—and maybe even funny or a little sexy, on our best days.

As humans, we hunger for so many things that extend beyond physical appetite. We hunger to know and to be known. We hunger for others to accept, understand, and adore us. We hunger to have someone to love and cherish with our affection. Knowing we were created this way, I began to suspect that food was created not just to satiate our bellies as we gather around the table but to create a place where God could meet us and fill our hearts. I started investigating the meaning and purpose of appetite in the Scripture.

As it turns out, food plays a major role in the pages of the Bible. Long before Rachael Ray learned to eat on forty dollars a day and Michael Pollan outlined the dilemma we omnivores face, God was the original foodie.

THE BIBLE'S DELICIOUS FIRST COURSE

The creation narrative in Genesis unfolds like a feast with fruits and vegetables everywhere. Birds fill the tree branches, fish school in the sea, and livestock roam free. Less than a thousand words into the Bible and God has already crafted every ingredient needed for an epic meal, so he takes the next logical step and creates someone to eat the fruits and veggies of this delicious bounty.

God handcrafted humanity to be dependent on food. The Creator could have required us to survive on air or water apart from eating, but He designed the human body so food is not an option but a necessity.

Even more delicious, God creates food as a source of pleasure. One of the marvels of our bodies is that we come equipped with between 2,000 and 10,000 taste buds, each one harboring 50 to 100 receptors that distinguish between the five main flavors: salty, bitter, sweet, sour, and umami (savory—think ripe tomatoes or shitake mushrooms). The tongue could exist without these nubbins, but God imbues us with the ability to delight in eating.

But food in the Bible is more than a commodity to be consumed. It is often sacred and symbolic, showing up both on tables and in temples. Food plays a prominent role in the most spiritually significant events from the moment the story starts.

In Genesis, the first humans take delectable strolls with the Creator in the bountiful Garden of Eden. I imagine the first couple plucking raspberries and peeling tangerines as they enjoy togetherness with God in the cool of the day. In Eden, God consecrates the first farm-to-table dining experience.

Then the sweetness of the story comes to an end in a bite of fruit, of all things. Much like us today, the couple want what they can't have and reach for the forbidden. With a few chews and chomps, their lives derail.

As Adam and Eve are removed from the garden buffet, God unfolds a blueprint to draw humanity back to himself. And—once again—our daily diets are involved. Food plays a significant role in helping us taste and see God's goodness in our lives. Everyday edibles become both a source of sustenance and sacred symbols. They often take on a spiritual dimension, a physical representation of God's grace and provision. And something beautiful happens when we gather around the table.

For the remainder of Genesis, a primary symbol of God's blessing is—you guessed it—food. Tasty treats spring up throughout the book. God uses Noah to preserve food in the ark and establishes his covenant with Abraham over a meaty offering. Abraham's wife, Sarah, bakes up bread cakes for angelic visitors and their son, Isaac, breathes a sigh of relief when roasted ram appears on the menu as a substitute offering. Later, Esau trades his blessing for lentil soup, and Jacob tricks his father into giving the blessing with goat stew. When famine threatens the globe, Joseph blesses all who come to him by feeding them. In this act, he foreshadows a day when the Son of God will bless all who come to him by feeding them the Bread of Life.

Food plays a significant role in helping us taste and see God's goodness in our lives.

The story of God's people continues with Moses and his sidekick brother, Aaron, whose staff produces miracles *and* wild almonds. When the dynamic duo face off against Pharaoh, who has enslaved the Israelites, Moses pronounces ten plagues on Egypt. The list reverses the Genesis creation order and decimates the food sources of Egypt, including livestock, poultry, fish, vegetables, fruit—even the water.

After their escape, the great Israelite exodus is memorialized through a delectable meal of sacred remembrance. Roasted lamb, bitter herbs, and flatbread still adorn Jewish tables each year as a means of passing the harrowing story on to future generations.

Once freed from Egypt, the Israelites receive a forty-year sabbatical in the Sinai desert, a barren place where food is difficult to find. Less than a fifty-day journey from Egypt, the Israelites awake in the wilderness of Sin (yes, that's really the name). They're willing to barter their newfound freedom for memories of food from an animal flesh-pot and hard, stale bread back in Egypt. Perhaps we shouldn't be surprised. They probably developed a taste for these in utero or as infants. They craved the comfort of the only life they had ever known.

The Lord persists in displaying his loving affection to the grumblers by providing food. One of the first courses on the menu arrives during a stopover in Elim where God's people drink from twelve springs of water and enjoy the natural candy of seventy date palm trees.

God soon sprinkles the desert with "manna." You won't find this sweet bread of heaven in aisle seven, but it's prominently displayed in the book of Exodus. Since humans cannot live on bread alone, God also rains down quail on the Israelites. The book of Numbers says the poultry reached a yard high as far as anyone can walk in a day. To translate the scene into classic Forrest Gump terms—you can barbecue it, boil, it, broil it, bake it, sauté it. There are quail kabobs, quail creole, quail gumbo. Pan-fried, deep-fried, stir-fried. There's pineapple quail, lemon quail, coconut quail, pepper quail, quail soup, quail stew, quail salad, quail and potatoes, quail burgers, quail sandwiches. God is the first foodie, but he apparently loves a good buffet too.

The divine menu of the desert sets the table for daily worship and adoration of God—dependence for every meal, trust for every step, a pathway to joy. During those years, the Israelites are tempted to lose heart and give up hope, but God promises he is cooking up something delectable for them and uses mealtime for their spiritual formation. In the hands of the Great Chef, food provides more than nourishment. It becomes a doorway to the divine and the gateway to transformation.

Through food, the Israelites will break free from their unhealthy upbringing.

Through food, the Israelites will grow in dependence on and trust in God.

Through food, the Israelites will discover new ways to think and talk about God.

Through food, the Israelites will experience the goodness of God together.

The story of the Israelites challenges us to be expectant for God to do the same in us whenever we gather around the table.

THE BIBLE'S DELECTABLE NEXT COURSE

When God bursts through the swinging doors of silence separating the Old and New Testaments, it's a buffet all over again. Jesus uses a variety of foodstuff to teach spiritual lessons. He compares the kingdom to wheat fields and bountiful banquets, and mountain-moving faith to a mustard seed. The Jesus we meet not only dies on a cross, but he also picks wheat, craves figs, and commands fish to be caught in Galilean nets.

Jesus's first miracle is a culinary conversion of water into wine at a wedding banquet, and later he feeds thousands with a basket of barley loaves and a handful of fish.

Mealtimes provide an opportunity for Jesus to gather his disciples and introduce them to the kingdom of God. Often the way Jesus consumes food and who he eats it with angers the religious establishment. They appear baffled when Jesus eats with unwashed hands, and they rage over the sketchy people who pull up a chair—tax collectors, prostitutes, and other "sinners."

Many of Jesus's most famous stories center around food as well. There's the one about the prodigal son who hopes to fill his stomach with pig slop but ends up with a steak dinner. And the beggar Lazarus who longs to eat from the rich man's table. And the parables about the vineyard workers and the rich man who stockpiles grain, unaware his life will soon end.

Crucial conversations, including the defense of Mary of Bethany with

her alabaster jar and even Judas's betrayal, take place surrounded by food. On the night of his betrayal, Jesus offers his disciples a spiritual practice that they should continue until he returns: a holy supper. And let's not forget the moment when the disciples who walk the road to Emmaus alongside the risen Christ have their eyes opened . . . as they break bread.

Jesus reveals himself as foodstuff: the bread of life, the true vine, the one anointed with olive oil, the sacrificial lamb. The Son of God is even described as someone who knocks on the doors of our souls, so we'll invite him in for supper. And when this whole shindig reaches its culmination, God handpicks the menu for the best banquet of all time—one that supersedes anything Adam and Eve experienced in Eden. Though food played a role in the fall, it plays a bigger role in God's redemptive plan.

> Jesus reveals himself as foodstuff: the bread of life, the true vine, the one anointed with olive oil, the sacrificial lamb.

If the God of the Bible uses food to open his people to divine possibility, and God is the same yesterday, today, and forever, then it stands to reason that God wants to do the same with us now.

A RECIPE FOR A RICHER RELATIONSHIP WITH GOD

The design of our modern world makes it easy to miss mealtime blessings. With harried schedules, many of us find ourselves grabbing anything that can be thrown inside a wrap, on a bun, or over a bed of lettuce. The meal, whether wolfed down behind a desk or behind the wheel, may be tasty but not memorable. Yet a blessing awaits whenever we carve out an appointed time to gather together and become fully present with God and one another. When we hold hands and give thanks and remember those who planted, harvested, and prepared the meal, we reconnect with ourselves and each other as humans made in the image of God.

Pause for a moment and ask, "What am I hungry for?" No, I don't mean nacho cheese Doritos or Häagen-Dazs peppermint bark bars. What are you *really* hungry for? When you gather around a table with those you most love and are most loved by, with those you know best and who know you best, what do you hope will be served? A savory entrée and a satisfying dessert, sure, but what are the unseen menu items you're hoping will appear as you're together?

Sometimes, in times of scarcity, we can be literally starving. But other times, our deepest hungers may seem more metaphorical or existential. Around the table, we discover something about longing. We recognize our need for someone to look us in the eye and truly see us, for someone to lean in and listen to us, for someone to nod and acknowledge that we're not alone. We may need someone to laugh at our jokes, tell us when we have spinach trapped in our teeth, or ask, "How are you *really* doing?"

When we gather to eat, God wants to nourish more than our bodies: he wants to nourish our souls with transcendent joy and supernatural community and divine presence. When we feed our physical appetites in community, we open our hearts for God to feed something deeper as well. He has connected our bodies and bellies to our spirits and souls. That, it seems, is the way God has designed us. God created us to give and receive, not just in our bodies but in our spirits.

The psalmist invites: "Taste and see that the LORD is good." Through these two sensory expressions, we are invited to become more attentive to God and the everyday aromatic, savory, and tactile expressions of his love.

Maybe you've never considered the Bible a book about food. I hadn't for most of my life. A tool to recognize God's voice in your life? Sure. An encouraging guide to awaken to the wonder of God?

Of course. A road map for a more joyful relationship with God? Definitely. But a foodie road map? Not a chance. An opportunity to think about the deep hungers of my life? Nope.

Once I realized the spiritual significance of food in the Bible, I decided to zero in on six foods that God uses to reveal and heal our deepest hungers. Since I'm not a food expert, only an aspiring foodie, I wanted to spend time with people who know these foods intimately, whose lives and livelihoods intertwine with these delicacies and could help me recognize Christ in their craft.

As always, God answered my prayer in the most unexpected ways. This expedition took me fishing in the Sea of Galilee, plucking figs in the farm belt of California, and baking fresh matzo at Yale University. I descended 420 feet into a Utah salt mine, harvested olives along the Croatian coast, and graduated from a Steakology 101 course in Texas.

What you hold in your hands is an invitation to take this adventure with me. This book is a spiritual travel and food guide designed to ensure you never read the Bible the same way again . . . you never approach the table the same way again . . . you never see food the same way again.

In hunger and fullness, may we draw closer to the one who fashioned us. More than a journey of food, this is a journey of faith, one designed to nourish our bellies and heal our souls. Let us taste and see God's goodness together. Let us follow our hunger and see what's cooking.

The table is set, drinks are poured, the meal is ready.

Pull up a chair.

Bon appétit and let's eat.

A Flaky Filet of Fish

TASTE AND SEE GOD'S POWER

I'm 6,941 miles from home on the southern rim of the Sea of Galilee, slogging through the marsh in rubber waders that I borrowed from a stranger. Israeli fishermen lay a gillnet in waist-deep water before me. They shout at each other in what I assume is Hebrew, but what my ears fail to hear, my eyes understand clearly. They have determined to fill their boats with St. Peter's fish. I am the only woman in the bunch—a female Bible teacher from America, no less—and one of the men is stripped down to his underwear.

How did I get myself in this mess?

The month prior, I had decided to throw myself into a study of food in the Bible, and my expedition would be incomplete without an exploration of fish. I prayed a (big) prayer that I'd meet the right people at the right time, and soon one divine encounter led to another. Thanks to my friend Christine, I connected with an Israeli man named Ido (pronounced Eee-dough). He grew up in Tiberias, on the edge of the Galilee in Israel, and now works as a jack-of-all-trades for his family's restaurants and boat tours.

"If I travel to Tiberias, will you take me fishing on the Galilee?" I asked after explaining how I got his number.

"Of course," he assured with a thick Israeli accent. Ido had a community of friends who were lifelong fishermen, and they would take us on their boats.

Now I had a decision to make: I could play it safe and learn about fish somewhere closer to home. Or I could take a risk and fly halfway around the world by myself (I'm not known for my street smarts) to meet a man that I didn't know (I flunked out of kickboxing) in a country that's a powder keg of geopolitical tension (my husband tends to worry).

Leif raised every possible concern, but in the end said he would support my decision to go. (He knew what he was signing up for when he said, "I do.") That was all my inner-adventurer needed to hear. Two clicks on the trackpad, and my itinerary was set.

As we counted down the days until takeoff, Leif and I could feel our shared anxiety rise. I'm stepping into a scenario in which anything can happen and, as much as I crave adventure, I confess I don't like being out of control. So I arm myself with a plan of all I want to accomplish, and on the morning of my departure, with nerves afire, Leif wraps me in his arms and whispers, "God, make a way so your power and presence may be seen by all."

After multiple plane changes between Salt Lake City and Tel Aviv, I rent a car and soon pull into Lido Beach on the shores of the Galilee. Built around a shady harbor, the Lido compound hosts a fleet of boats and two restaurants, the Pagoda and the famed

Decks, which attract everyone from dignitaries to Jewish families celebrating bat and bar mitzvahs.

A six-foot-four man wearing a black T-shirt and jeans emerges from behind a gate carrying a mug of tea in each hand. With bluish eyes, a shaved head, and deep laugh lines, he is a dead ringer for Bruce Willis.

Ido carries himself with an affable gait and gregarious grin. Knowing the sharing of food is an act of friendship in Middle Eastern culture, I accept the piping cup of licorice tea as Ido leads me on a tour of his family's property. He highlights everything he has made by hand—custom chairs and tables, guardrails and concrete decks, even the grills in the kitchen. He's a high-energy Jewish Renaissance man.

He ushers me toward the docks, where he points out his latest project: a fiberglass replica of the Ancient Galilee Boat, also known as "The Jesus Boat," to take pilgrims on tours. Discovered four miles away from Lido in 1986, the wooden vessel dates to the first century AD and provides insights into the watercraft used during Jesus's lifetime.

Twenty-seven feet in length and seven-and-a-half feet wide, its flat bottom and shallow draft allow the vessel to inch close for inshore fishing. The boat, with its four staggered rowers and a mast for sailing, could adapt to the ever-changing weather conditions on the lake. A cooking pot and lamp found inside the vessel confirm the fishermen worked late into the night and prepared meals aboard their boats just as they do today.

I remember the scene in Mark's Gospel when a sudden squall catches the disciples off-guard. The waves crash over the boat until it's nearly swamped. Yet, amazingly, Jesus dozes on a cushion in the aft. When I see the shape and dimensions of the original discovery, as well as Ido's re-creation, I grasp both the credibility and the absurdity of the scene.

The Sea of Galilee is relatively shallow, just 200 feet at its deepest point. The result is that wind stirs up the water more readily because the energy cannot be absorbed as quickly as with deeper lakes. As a result, the waves on the lake are abnormally close together. Vessels, especially of this size, would be tossed with more severity during a storm. The scene of Jesus snoozing seems outrageous with a backdrop of disciples straining at the oars, gusts of wind screaming, gallons of saline breaking over the bow. Yet Christ slumbers in peace.

Even more shocking: Jesus's power to calm a raging sea that's thirty-three miles in diameter with the words, "Quiet! Be still."

Though I find the Ancient Galilee Boat fascinating, I haven't traveled halfway around the world to study vessels as much as fish.

"When can we go fishing?" I ask eagerly.

"Yah, yah, we go," Ido hushes. "But first I must buy wood. You come?"

Since Passover is days away, Ido has many projects to complete before the city shuts down. Without much choice, I scrunch in the cab of the truck alongside his workers and son.

The next thing I know, I'm standing in the middle of a field more than an hour's drive away as Ido negotiates the purchase of an enormous trunk of a Jerusalem pine. Somewhere in the foreign conversation with the sellers I hear the English phrase, "Feinberg Wood Industries." Later, Ido explains that he introduced me as a wood dealer from America to negotiate a better price for the special table he's building in the restaurant. When I question his business ethics, he laughs and says it's all just play.

We don't go fishing that day . . . or the next three days. Every morning I ask about fishing and Ido answers, "But first I must . . ."

Then we leave on another work-related errand that involves buying, selling, and most important, negotiating. Ido assures me that his friends rank among the best fishermen on the lake. They will take us. This was not the fishing-palooza trip I envisioned—at all—and I wondered what God had in store for me instead.

At the end of the fourth day, after we headed away from the lake yet again, Ido has introduced me as a filmmaker from Los Angeles, a journalist for *National Geographic*, and an owner-operator of a glamping company. I am living on "Israeli time" and "Ido time," which means everything takes ten times as long.

Each day feels like I'm trapped in a Choose Your Own Adventure escapade, except Ido makes all the decisions. I follow behind like a kite tail whipped about in the wind.

The situation grates against my plans and well-worn desire to be in charge. Picking something as simple as your destination plays well into the illusion that destiny is yours to control; however, this trip has stripped me of making choices. A part of me is tempted to pack my bags and return home in frustration. Yet I sense that if I relinquish control and stop trying to set the agenda, maybe I'll make space for God to move.

I force myself to receive each day as a gift rather than manage it like a to-do list. It's a tussle, sometimes hour by hour, and with time, my experience begins to shift.

The unexpected detours of our adventures include stops at a goat farm, an olive orchard, a Bedouin's cattle herd, and fields of fig trees, vines, and wheat. As I relent to the uncharted tour, I am able to pay closer attention to each experience. I learn something insightful at each stop and start to trust in this non-plan plan. In the evenings, the entire family gathers around the table—Ido's wife, Yael; his four children, Erez, Peleg, Ella, and Gefen; his mother, Vered; and his grandmother, Esther, who, like all Jewish grandmothers, shovels more food on my plate every time I look away.

As we eat together, Ido recounts the day's adventures. The events which are curious and comical to me appear normal to everyone else. Ido's wife, Yael, provides the only hints of oversight to the beautiful chaos. We clap when five-year-old Ella, who has long lost interest in food, plays dress-up with yet another outfit. And we watch two-year-old Gefen return to the table every few minutes with a new toy. Listening to young Jewish children call their father "Abba" is especially moving. I find myself enmeshed in the daily food, cooking, and life of a Jewish family in ways I never imagined.

But I don't lose sight that I've come here for fish. So late into the evenings, I study the Hebrew Bible to reel in fresh insights.

HOW FISH SWIM THROUGH THE BIBLE

The Torah, the first five books of the Old Testament, teems with fish. They arrive on the fifth day of creation when God stocks the seas with marine creatures. Soon after, Adam goes on a naming spree of the livestock and birds and wild animals, but alas, the fish don't make the list. Some suggest with lightheartedness that's why only one word exists for fish in the Hebrew Bible—*dag*—which covers all species.

The Egyptians pioneered the art of fishing. Though planted in the desert, they engineered an extensive labyrinth of aqueducts along the Nile, which allowed them to serve catfish, mullet, carp, and moonfish. Yet Pharaoh's refusal to heed Moses's warning to release the Israelites ruins their supply. God displays his power when the waters turn bloody red and the stench of hundreds of thousands of fish carcasses bitters the air.

Pharaoh agrees to liberate the Israelites, but he proves to be a double-crosser. Shortly after their evacuation, the Egyptian army chases God's people into the Red Sea—their only path of escape. As soon as they make it safely to the other side, the parted waters crash down on the Egyptians. Their bloated bodies soon wash up on the shores, likely after fish nibbled on a few toes.

The Israelites' gratitude wanes and they soon find themselves underwhelmed, flooding God's ears with complaint. They miss Egyptian food—especially those fresh fish sticks.

In faithfulness, grace, and love, God leads them to the Promised Land, which includes a fisherman's paradise along the banks of the Galilee and the shores of the Mediterranean. Yet Moses knows their wandering hearts and issues a stern warning in the desert: wherever you go, don't worship any fish.

While such a command sounds strange to modern ears, one of the strongest factions in the land, the Philistines, worship a fish-god known as Dagon. When the Philistines capture the ark of the Lord from the Israelites during the period of the judges, they carry it into Dagon's temple. Their idol appears face down the next day. They set him upright. Dagon's head and appendages break off by the next morning. They set him upright again. Soon tumors appear all over their bodies. After so many displays of God's power, the Philistines cry out to let God's ark go.

The story is a reminder that worshipping false gods will make you the chicken of the sea.

Fish are beloved by the Israelites because the addition of a sardine or fish sauce is a treat that breaks up the monotony of the bread, bread, bread and more bread in the ancient diet.

As a literal sign of their culinary preferences, "The Fish Gate" becomes one of the famed entrances into Jerusalem. Much like the

Pike Place Market in Seattle, the name signifies its geographic location, specifically its proximity to fish peddlers selling their daily catches. Six days a week, the fishermen sell their fish transported from the Mediterranean and the Galilee.

The Scripture notes multiple occasions when God's people fill their bellies with fish, but then there's that time when a fish is filled with one of God's prophets! Jonah starts in the bowels of a ship and ends up in the bowels of a big fish. Three stinky days later, Jonah parks on the beach, covered in fish sneeze. The prophet plucks seaweed from his beard, then delivers what may be the shortest, most effective sermon in history: "Forty more days and Nineveh will be overthrown." With those words, all the Ninevites fast, wear sackcloth, and return to God.

Table Discovery: Rather than shop for a specific type of fish the next time you go to the market, ask the clerk for the freshest fish available. Recipes that call for tilapia can be substituted with other mild tasting fish like cod or snapper. Look for firm filets without discoloration. If you're purchasing a whole fish, look for clear eyes and tight scales on the skin.

Other prophets, including Isaiah, Jeremiah, Amos, and Zephaniah, all use fish imagery in communicating God's heart to his people. The frequent mentions suggest they're well-acquainted with the occupation of fishermen.

Yet it's Ezekiel who makes one of the strangest prophecies when he describes a great abundance of fish from an unlikely source: where the water from Jerusalem meets the Dead Sea. Everyone knows the Dead Sea is famous for being, well, dead. Nothing lives in it. So how is this possible?

In the midst of exile, the prophet describes a time when life will flow from Jerusalem once again. The temple will no longer be a place of corruption but a source of life. The miracle is the fresh water flowing from the temple creating an environment for abundance. Turns out when fresh water meets salt water, an estuary of brackish water forms. The level of salinity changes, creating a place where fish gather and thrive. The prophet proclaims that nothing is impossible when the power of God is involved.

With so many fish swimming throughout the ancient text, I can't wait to dive into the Gospels. But first I need to ensure I haven't traveled this far to return home without a catch.

THE SECRET TO CATCHING A ST. PETER'S FISH

By day five, Ido can sense my restlessness.

"Today, we go fishing," he announces.

I only half-believe him. But that afternoon we drive to the southern shore of the Galilee. I climb aboard a beaten, pale-blue fiberglass skiff with a small engine and two narrow rectangular oars. Sun-worn tarps cover a pile of nets in the center of the boat.

As we pull away from the jetty, Ido points to splashes on the shore. Large fish appear stacked atop each other against the bank.

"Catfish mating season," Ido says. "We don't eat them. Know why?"

I shake my head.

"We're Jewish."

Only then do I remember the parable in which Jesus compares the kingdom of heaven to a net let down in a lake. Once full, the fishermen pull their catch to shore and separate the good fish from the bad. Thanks to Ido, I now know the bad fish are the catfish. Because they lack scales, they are considered unclean. That's why they're the biggest fish in the sea. If you're a catfish lover, world-class fishing awaits on the shores of the Galilee.

After a short boat ride, we meet up with another skiff. Shlomo, known as "Momo," is the owner and operator of a pair of boats with a crew of four, including himself. All the men wear a white T-shirt and matching navy-blue fishing waders. Their leathery skin and muscular frames are chiseled by their profession as they work six days a week, while resting on the Sabbath.

Neither Momo nor his crew speak English, so Ido translates. Momo has fished these waters for thirty-seven years and claims to know every inch of the Sea of Galilee. I don't doubt him. He explains that the fish migrate toward the south of the sea in the winter and to the north in the summer.

A hundred yards from shore, Momo signals for his men to drop a net. The engine stops, and we wait for stillness to set in. The waters calm, and I recognize why he's chosen this precise location. I peer over the edge and notice a large log that attracts fish to its shadows.

Momo's right-hand man lifts a tarp to uncover a trammel net, known as an *ambaten* in Hebrew. He releases the layered net, with metal weights on the bottom and red floaters on the top, to form a vertical wall in the water. Meanwhile, Momo uses the oars to row the boat one hundred yards across and then inward five times to create a spiral formation.

Once in the center, the secondary boat sculls around us. A crew-man uses a toilet plunger to shock the water with loud sounds. The ruckus compels the fish to dive to the bottom, where they entangle in the net. The same method, the slapping of oars, has been used on the Galilee for thousands of years.

Then we sit in silence. Momo scans the surface. A bobble on a floater signifies a trapped fish. He points to a second with a half-grin. Momo announces, "Ya!" and the crewmen retrieve the net. The crew cheers when the first St. Peter's fish, a kind of tilapia, flops inside a cooler.

The one-pound silver fish has a long dorsal fin resembling a comb. The Hebrew name for St. Peter's fish is *amnon,* meaning "nurse fish" because the parents store their eggs in their mouths for two to three weeks until the eggs hatch, then watch over them afterward—an unusual, nurturing act for a cold-blooded creature.

The fish gets its nickname from a popular story in Matthew. The disciples arrive in the fishing village of Capernaum. A tax collector approaches Peter, because, at the time, every Jewish adult male must pay two drachma as a temple tax equivalent to a day's wage. To test Jesus's loyalty, the Pharisees ask Peter whether Jesus pays the tax. Peter insists Jesus is an upstanding taxpayer.

When Peter arrives home, Jesus greets him with a question: "From whom do the kings of the earth collect duty and taxes—from their own children or from others?"

"From others," Peter answers.

"Then the children are exempt," Jesus says. "But so that we may not cause offense, go to the lake and throw out your line. Take the first fish you catch; open its mouth and you will find a four-drachma coin. Take it and give it to them for my tax and yours."

Not only do the wind and the waves cater to Jesus's command, but the fish also.

Much like Jonah emerging from a fish's mouth, this stunning act displays God's power over creation. Not only do the wind and the waves cater to Jesus's command, but the fish also.

The supernatural story is remembered whenever restaurant guests order a baked, broiled, or fried "St. Peter's fish." The only problem, from the perspective of local fishermen: this isn't the breed of fish Peter caught.

The St. Peter's fish feeds only on plankton, so catching the famous fish requires nets, not hooks. The fish Peter most likely pulled from the waters is the carp-like barbel, famed for the barbs on the corners of its mouth and commonly caught with a line.

The amnon probably earned the name St. Peter's fish because it's the best-tasting fish in the sea. The name change was simply good for tourism, and that's why it remains a must-eat meal for visitors to the region.

When Momo's crewmen finish retrieving the net, a handful of fish flop in the cooler. Ido appears thrilled by the variety—a pair of St. Peter's fish and three different species of barbels. But Momo shakes his head in disappointment. The barbels earn forty cents a pound *if* you can find someone to buy them, whereas the St. Peter's fish bring in two to four dollars a pound. When your livelihood depends on the sea and you and your employees labor for an hour to catch only two sellable fish, it's a net loss.

But Momo refuses to give up.

He rows the boat toward the marshy shore, climbs out of the vessel, and walks in chest-deep water toward land, his eyes sweeping the surface for fish. From the rocky beach, he squints toward us, calling out in Hebrew.

The fishermen spring into action. They climb into the water with floating coolers filled with nets. In an act of kindness, one of the crewmen loans me his fishing waders. There's not an extra pair for Ido. He strips down to his skivvies that look like Israeli lederhosen.

We march through the waters as the nets are lowered and linked to create a half-mile wall between the beach and the deeper water. Once the nets are set, a crewman plunges into the water to drive the fish into the wall.

I offer to take the plunger but am told there's too much at stake. I try not to get in their way, snapping as many photos as I can without dropping my phone to its watery grave.

So that's how I end up 6,941 miles away from home, slogging through watery marsh with four men who don't speak a lick of English—and a fifth in his underwear.

Two hours later, when Momo and his men retrieve the nets, they haul in 150 pounds of St. Peter's fish, well above and beyond the tiny catch they snagged earlier. That's when I realize that the one on the beach recognizes something we cannot from the boats.

And from a heavenly vantage point, God always sees what we cannot.

How often I forget this in my spiritual life. When we rely on our own power, our eyes set on the goal. When we relinquish control, we become free to fix our eyes on God. Sometimes I become so obsessed with what's before me, on the five meager fish in my cooler—or on a trip that isn't following my original plan—that I fail to shift my gaze to the One who sees all things, who holds all things together, who remains all-powerful.

This tendency becomes more acute when, like the fishing crew with a near-empty catch, I'm exhausted and frustrated and disappointed. In those moments I need the One who calls to the disciples from the shore. The One whose perspective is more expansive, whose ways are higher, whose plan is better, whose power is limitless.

Yet my spiritual eyes are only beginning to open to all God is revealing.

By the time we return to the harbor, Ido convinces Momo to give us the five fish from the original catch. I wait for Ido to drum up my next exaggerated career, but this time he tells the truth—I'm an author exploring food and the Bible. They seem just fine with that.

Later that evening, we gather around the family table once again enjoying the food and one another. I'm grateful for the fish and especially the fishing expedition. Mama Vered peppers me with questions about the experience. She's proud of Ido for bringing home dinner.

The barbels, the less tasty choice, become a popular Jewish dish known as gefilte fish, which tastes like a slab of fishy meatloaf. I'm grateful I only took a small chunk. But this is one of Grandmother Esther's favorite foods from childhood, so she goes back for seconds and thirds. I haven't seen her eat this much any other night.

The prized St. Peter's fish is served in a more familiar fashion. It's broiled and served with an oversized, charred sweet potato. The fish's thin skin peels away to reveal a flaky white filet, and the bones separate with ease. The gentle flavor comes alive with a twist of fresh lemon as the meat melts in my mouth.

If you're ever given the choice between the two dishes, I recommend the St. Peter's fish every time.

THE FISHING STORY YOU THOUGHT YOU KNEW

My time with Momo and his crew on the boat proves invaluable, yet I glean as much from sitting on the shore, watching men cast nets along the docks and rocks, observing the changing weather patterns, and interacting with those who fish when they return to the harbor.

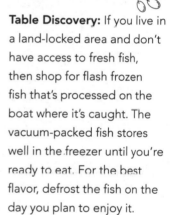

Before visiting Israel, the Sea of Galilee, also known as the Sea of Tiberias and Lake of Gennesaret in the Gospels, always sounded enormous to me. One rare lazy afternoon during my visit, I drive its perimeter in an hour. Afterward, Ido gushes that he knows "a fox of a driver" who can do it in twenty-seven minutes.

Jesus could have settled anywhere after leaving Nazareth. Yet he claims the shores of this harp-shaped lake as home. Here he launches his earthly ministry amid the boats and harbors. He handpicks fishermen as his first disciples. Jesus asks his followers to give their most valuable possessions: their livelihoods. Their boats, once used for profitable businesses, transform into floating pulpits and provide much-needed transportation. The nets now do more than form a wall for fish; they break down walls in people's hearts. The linen netting becomes an instrument for expanding people's understanding of the power of God.

Table Discovery: If you live in a land-locked area and don't have access to fresh fish, then shop for flash frozen fish that's processed on the boat where it's caught. The vacuum-packed fish stores well in the freezer until you're ready to eat. For the best flavor, defrost the fish on the day you plan to enjoy it.

One of the questions I most enjoy asking fishermen is about their best catch ever. Momo recalls an afternoon when his crew set their nets near Lido and worked all day. By evening, they brought in 2.1 tons of fish—the most he's ever seen. Ido describes hauling in a 670-pound tuna from the depths of the Mediterranean with his handmade gaff. Fishermen, by nature, are people whose big fish tales spread fast. No wonder so many fish miracles fill the Gospels.

Yet it's our doctor friend, Luke, who paints the most detailed pictures of how Jesus interrupted life on the shores of the Galilee.

After a long night's work, a fishing crew returns to the harbor in the mornings. Without access to modern, clear, synthetic netting, they depend on a cotton-based linen for net-making. The white strands are easily detectable to the fish in daylight hours, so the men always venture out at night. In Luke's story, the men return at dawn without any fish.

For fishermen, the return to port doesn't end when the boat docks. They must still wash, mend, and dry the nets to prevent mildew. Then they wrap them in a sheltering cloth to prevent sun damage.

In this instance, Jesus approaches and the fishing boats sit empty. The crewmen busy themselves repairing and washing the nets on shore. Jesus climbs into an unoccupied vessel and asks Simon Peter to push out the boat. Then he instructs, "Put out into deep water, and let down the nets for a catch."

Remember, the disciples have already worked all night. They know it's a waste of time and energy to set a linen dragnet during the day.

"But because you say so, I will let down the nets," Simon Peter obliges.

One of the empty gourds, commonly used as floaters in antiquity, bobbles in the water. The men perk with excitement. Soon all the floaters dance. Peter flashes the signal to retrieve the net. Fish wiggle in the webbing until they create frays. Some lucky fish scoot away.

Simon Peter calls out to his partners, the sons of Zebedee, for extra hands. Soon both vessels become so weighed down with the enormous catch, they take on water. They return to shore with the most lucrative haul of their entire lives. Simon Peter can't believe his eyes. The unlimited power of God displays itself in the nets, and even more in the person before him. He falls at Jesus's knees and begs for his life. "Master, leave. I'm a sinner and can't handle this holiness. Leave me to myself."

Jesus refuses to budge and assures Peter that in the wake of his power there's nothing to fear: he's not going anywhere. Once ashore, Simon Peter, Andrew, James, and John leave everything and follow Jesus.

We read this famous fishing story today with the advantage of knowing that those boats and nets will serve a purpose again. But in the moment, the disciples believe they're leaving them forever. They give up their transportation, their livelihoods, their futures, not to mention the biggest catch of their lives. They've just won the fishing lottery, but they leave it behind for something far better. Scripture doesn't tell us who cashed in that astounding catch. But the disciples' sacrifices become the very things Jesus uses to display his power and glory. This is the first miracle the disciples witness in their boats. The Son of God unleashes his power in the midst of their daily routine, their daily work, their daily chores.

Because this mighty act occurs far from us on a map, we can start to think God prefers to move in faraway places. We can fall into the belief that God performs his greatest works in other locations, in other people, in other situations. We forget that Jesus wants to show up in our lives—here, now, today.

The disciples' stories remind us this isn't a once-in-a-lifetime occurrence. Throughout their travels with Jesus, they encounter so many remarkable displays of God's power they can't write them all down.

So it's no surprise that Jesus makes his grand exit in a similar fashion as his entrance. After his death and resurrection, the original fishermen return to their familiar livelihoods.

In the final chapter of John's Gospel, Peter and the Zebedee brothers fish all night but catch nothing. Once again, Jesus comes to people disappointed in their work. Jesus calls from the shores of the Galilee to his friends who don't recognize him. He instructs them to throw their nets into the water, this time on the right side of the boat, perhaps because they're already in deep water.

The gourds dance, the nets overflow, and a few fish scuttle away.

The Gospel of John describes that after the fishermen haul their nets to shore, Jesus greets them with breakfast on the beach. One can imagine the allure of fresh baked bread and fish broiled over charcoal wafting through the air. Jesus asks the disciples to bring some of their catch, not because he doesn't have enough, but because he has something else in mind.

I always thought the early-morning breakfast lesson was that even though God has everything, we are still invited to be participatory givers. While this remains true, after my time on the Galilee, I see it anew.

The disciples haul their seine nets ashore but still have hours of work ahead to disentangle all the fish, wash, mend, and dry their nets. Yet they leave their nets for an opportunity to break bread with the Bread of Life.

Only one disciple responds to Jesus's request for more fish. The last time this disciple saw Jesus, he stood near a charcoal fire, too—and proceeded to deny Jesus three times.

Proud as ever, Peter refuses to repeat the same mistake.

"So Simon Peter climbed back into the boat and dragged the net ashore. It was full of large fish, 153, but even with so many the net was not torn."

When Peter returns to the boats, he doesn't disentangle fish from the nets already on shore. Instead, he climbs into the boat and likely reaches for a new net—a cast net, which is the only kind of net that can be handled by one man. He tosses it in the water and hauls in more than a gross of large fish, and among them his namesake, the St. Peter's Fish.

Mendel Nun, a fishing expert in this region, suggests there were multiple catches on that day. The first catch with the disciples and the second catch with Peter. Catching that many fish with different methods layers miracle on miracle.

Peter experiences Jesus's voltage in his life again through the abundant catch. These miracles provide the set-up for Peter's warm embrace and recommissioning by Christ.

Just as the disciples' first miraculous catch ushers them into an unforgettable journey with Christ, so too these catches launch them into uncharted adventure as faithful followers.

SURROUNDED BY MORE MIRACLES THAN YOU REALIZE?

On my final morning in Israel, I climb out of bed in darkness and make my way to the docks as the sun rises over the hillside. The birds, with their high shrills and steady chirps, form a choir in a nearby tree. Seagulls circle the harbor and pause mid-flight to make the occasional dive. A dog's bark echoes in the distance.

I realize that I had to uncurl my fingers from the trip I envisioned to make space for the adventure God had preplanned all along. I don't like being out of control—who does, really?—yet accepting our powerlessness is a sacred discipline.

When I relinquished, God flooded in and made himself known. I suspect he wants to do that a lot more than I allow. He longs to display his power and might in our lives, but he won't kick us off the throne if we're committed to wearing the crown of control.

The Sea of Galilee exudes a calmness that stills my soul. My eyes wander along the emerald coast. This is more than a spot where water meets land: it's where heaven intersected earth; where Jesus displayed the power of God to mere mortals.

To the north, Jesus once fed five thousand with five bricks of barley and a pair of sardines. A few miles away he repeated the miracle for four thousand.

A little further and Peter caught the carp that provided the temple tax.

My eyes scan the lake where Jesus calmed wicked storms, not once but twice. And upon these waters, Jesus strolled with ease.

I'm surrounded by grand displays of God's power. This landscape is marked by the miraculous in every direction.

This is easy to recognize when you're beside the Galilee, overlooking the waters where Jesus lived. But the experience isn't limited to people with the time and resources to make the trek to Israel.

Christ wants us to see these vistas in our daily lives. He wants us to awaken to all the places God unleashes mightiness—in our past and present, so we can look forward to a faith-filled future.

The provision supplied. The storms calmed. The relationships restored.

I catch this panorama in the ways God has sustained Leif and me. I remember the faces of those God has brought into my life to quell the pangs of loneliness. I look back to the many moves in my life and see how Jesus met and grew me through each one. I also remember the dark seasons, such as when the storm of financial ruin struck our lives; though it took years to repay, God provided all along the way. Then a cancer diagnosis that broke my body and my will, but even in that, God breathed new life.

If you look at your life through this panoramic lens, you'll recognize the powerful displays of God's presence through it all.

But if you stop looking to Jesus as your powerhouse, you may start thinking God is overlooking you, ignoring you, or worse yet, punishing you. If you close your eyes too long to God's presence, you may convince yourself that somehow God has rejected you, or worse, has abandoned you altogether. You'll grow deaf to the One who calls from the shore, the One who wants to fill your nets with the impossible and unimaginable.

Yet if you search your everyday life for the presence of Christ, you'll begin to see the extra provision, extra might, extra grace that he's slipping you. The way he provides an unexpected compliment from a friend. Or a familiar face that you weren't expecting in a crowded place. Or a breathtaking sunset. These displays of God's power are good and beautiful, like the fish the disciples caught. But the greatest miracle remains the One who sent them.

It's holy irony that the first letters of the Greek words "Jesus Christ, God's Son, Savior" form the word *ichthys,* meaning "fish" in Greek.

That's one reason early believers, amid persecution, chose the fish as their secret symbol. The common image didn't raise any suspicions yet carried the memories of Christ's power and calling to become "fishers of men." Archaeologists have discovered pictures of fish carved in the stone and painted on the walls where early Christ-followers gathered and prayed in secret.

It's even said that when a believer met a stranger in the road, the Christ-follower might draw an arc of a simple fish in the dirt. If the stranger drew the other arc to complete the fish, both knew they were in safe company.

For them and for us, the fish reminds us to live on high alert for the power of Christ to invade our daily lives in something as basic and everyday as our food.

The sun rises higher, and I know my time is coming to a close. I drag my finger through the sand of the shore, forming a fish. *Thank you, God, for your power,* I whisper.

When it's time to depart, I give Ido a bear hug to thank him for his hospitality. He seems sad to see me leave.

"I hope you got what you came for, Margaret," he offers.

"I got all I needed and so much more," I reply. "Only God could have orchestrated such an adventure."

And so it is with us all.

AROUND THE TABLE

At the end of each chapter, you'll find a simple activity to share around the table after a meal with friends, family, and soon-to-be friends.

For this chapter's activity, find an outline of the Sea of Galilee that you can photocopy, one per person. (If you'd like to download a free printable map to photocopy, simply visit www.margaretfeinberg.com/tasteandsee.) Now imagine you're sitting on the bank, looking around the coast at the miracles that Jesus has done in your life. People you met. Jobs you landed. Provision you needed. Healing you desired. Grace you experienced. On the map, note places around the lake where Jesus has displayed his power in your life. Then share some of these miracles with one another.

MOM'S ALMOND-CRUSTED TILAPIA

I grew up on a boat, and this fall-apart-in-your-mouth fish recipe will become a family favorite. Best served with roasted veggies or steamed rice.

PREP: 10 minutes   **COOK:** 4 minutes   **COOL:** none

4 tilapia filets
1 egg beaten with 1 teaspoon water
$1/2$ cup ground almonds
$1/2$ cup panko
$1/4$ cup grated Parmesan
$1/2$ teaspoon garlic salt
1 tablespoon olive oil
1 tablespoon butter
lemon and parsley for garnish

DIRECTIONS

1. Mix almonds, panko, parmesan, and garlic salt in small bowl.
2. Dip filets in egg mix. Press coating onto fish.
3. Sauté in olive oil and butter on one side until golden brown, about 2 minutes. Turn and cook another 2 minutes.
4. Garnish with lemon and parsley and enjoy.

Serves 2–4.

LEIF'S BAKED HALIBUT

My husband, Leif, is from Sitka, Alaska, and has cooked fish countless ways. This tasty recipe is best served with fresh vegetables, salad, and rice or baked potato.

PREP: 10 minutes   **COOK:** 25 minutes   **COOL:** 2 minutes

1-pound halibut filet, divided into four pieces
1/4 cup mayonnaise
1/4 cup Dijon mustard
1/2 cup grated cheddar cheese
salt and pepper to taste

DIRECTIONS

1. Preheat oven to 400 degrees.
2. Rinse fish, then salt and pepper both sides of the filets.
3. Mix mayonnaise and mustard.
4. Spray baking pan with oil. Place fish skin side down. Spread the mayonnaise and mustard mixture over the top of the fish. Sprinkle cheese evenly over the four pieces of fish.
5. Bake between 18–23 minutes until cheese melts and starts to brown. Fish should flake easily with a fork.

Serves 2–3.

LEIF'S SPICY SMOKED SALMON DIP

This tasty dip is best served with a variety of your favorite fresh veggies and bagel chips, made into a sandwich, or just eaten with a fork.

PREP: 10 minutes (more depending on veggies served with the dip)

COOK: none
COOL: none
8 ounces of cream cheese

4 ounces of smoked salmon (not canned in oil)

1/2 cup of plain Greek yogurt
1 tablespoon of fresh lemon juice
3 green onion sliced (reserve the whites for another use)
1/2 diced jalapeño or Sriracha sauce to taste
salt and pepper to taste
bread, crackers, or veggies to serve

DIRECTIONS

1. Using an electric mixer, blend the cream cheese until smooth.
2. Add the remaining ingredients and mix using a fork until well blended.
3. Taste and then season with salt and pepper and additional jalapeño or Sriracha.
4. Chill and then serve with bread, crackers, or veggies.

Makes 1 1/2 pints.

WES'S GRILLED FISH TACOS WITH BAJA SLAW

Fish tacos are a great addition to your weekly menu. They provide a fun and nutritious way to introduce kids to fish and consume healthy Omega-3s.

PREP: 45 minutes   **COOK:** 15 minutes   **COOL:** none

FISH:
1 pound of favorite fish (tilapia, snapper, or whatever is fresh or flash frozen)
2 tablespoons taco seasoning
2 tablespoons olive oil

BAJA SLAW:
3 cups shredded cabbage
1/2 cup mayonnaise
1/4 cup of sour cream
2 tablespoons Sriracha
1 tablespoon lime juice
1 tablespoon taco seasoning

TACO TOPPINGS:
1 8-ounce jar pico de gallo
salt and pepper to taste
Package of 6-inch corn tortillas
1 lime cut into 4 wedges
8 ounces shredded Mexican-style cheese

DIRECTIONS

1. To prepare the fish, pat dry with a paper towel and cut the filets into strips approximately 1 inch wide and 5 inches long. Add 2 tablespoons of your favorite taco seasoning and 2 tablespoons of olive oil. Mix gently to evenly coat all sides of the strips. Let sit for 15 minutes.
2. While the fish is resting, prepare the Baja Slaw and preheat your grill to medium heat. Mix all ingredients for the Baja Slaw into a bowl, cover, and let sit in the refrigerator until ready to serve.
3. Place fish on aluminum foil on grill. Cook each side 4–5 minutes on medium heat until the fish is moist and flakey.
4. Heat tortillas on the stove top with a squeeze of lime.
5. Build your tacos with tortillas, slaw, cheese, lime, and extra Sriracha.

Serves 4.

A Plate of Sweet and Succulent Figs

TASTE AND SEE GOD'S SATISFACTION

After Leif and I moved to Salt Lake City from Colorado, I would often slip out on late-afternoon walks to explore our surrounding neighborhood where fruit trees dotted the streets. The sweet fragrance of their spring blossoms soon gave way to the ripening of apples and apricots, pears and plums. In nearby yards, grapes crawled along brick walls. I felt like I had arrived in a fruit lover's paradise.

I have always been a frugivore and can eat fruit for breakfast, lunch, dinner, and every snack between. So I started asking my new neighbors for permission to pick from their yards. "Gather as much as you want," they said, delighted to share the fruit rather than watch it rot on the ground. My exercise and mealtimes soon merged as my walks evolved into a multicourse menu. I savored a soft nectarine followed by a juicy plum, then made a beeline two blocks over for a honey-sweet apple. Six blocks farther and I would pluck a handful of flavor-bursting cherries for dessert. Each time I brought home another basket of foraged fruit, Leif would give me a look that murmured, *Here she goes again.*

What started out as delightful strolls turned into something more. When I mentioned my tasty capers to newfound friends, we formed a ragtag fruit-pickers club. Before I knew it, we were harvesting the neighborhood.

I never imagined the bonding that could happen as we explored backyards and parks gleaning unpicked fruit. Budding relation-ships blossomed. Many of my friends' children knew fruit only from the grocery produce section. Their eyes lit up when they realized they could pick fresh fruit and enjoy all the samples they wanted. The conversations felt natural as our hands stayed busy. Fresh juice dripped from our chins amid bursts of laughter. Our tummies and hearts filled, and our kitchens overflowed with tangy goodness. We experimented with recipes for apple pie, peach cob-bler, and a magical pear tart. We picked and baked and taste-tested and recipe-shared our way through the summer. By early fall I had established real friendships around these experiences. Fruit had brought us together.

As I set out to explore food in the Bible, I naturally took a fruit-forward approach and placed it toward the top of my list. I would never have predicted that the word *fruit* would appear almost two hundred times in Scripture (if you add *fruitful,* another three dozen mentions arise). The first hint of fruit in the Bible occurs, well, in the beginning. On the third day of creation, God handcrafts the trees to bear fruit according to their seed, and humanity has been enjoying the natural sugars ever since. The first humans commit the first sin by misusing—you guessed it—fruit.

As the Bible's narrative progresses, fruit continues appearing. God instructs the Israelites to give their "first fruits." And the Promised

Land sounds like a Zagat-rated, sugary buffet since five of the seven foods found there are technically fruits—figs, dates, pomegranates, grapes, and olives. (Sorry, wheat and barley.)

Until I scouted for fruit in the Bible, I never realized how much meaning could be picked from its pages, some of which I had overlooked my entire life. When a particular variety thrives in a region, a nearby town or city was often named after it. Carmel, the site of the famed showdown between Elijah and the false prophets, means "vineyard," and Anab, mentioned in Joshua, means "grape."

Suddenly I couldn't help noticing the significance behind fruit everywhere I went. Dates are one of the primary ingredients in my favorite protein bar, but I can't say I know how they grow. In the Bible, whenever palm trees appear, they're referring to date palms. The "City of Palms," later named Jericho, is an oasis surrounded by dates. When Jesus enters Jerusalem for Passover, people line the streets welcoming him with boughs of date palms. The fruit of these trees symbolizes victory over death. Whether or not the people recognized the prophetic nature of their actions, we don't know, but they set the stage for One who will soon conquer the grim reaper once and for all.

As for pomegranates, the stately fruit has an actual crown, a symbol of royalty that sits atop. God instructs that images of pomegranates should be positioned on the pillars outside of the holy of holies and the hemlines of the high priests' robes.

Grapevines snake through the pages of Scripture, too. God tells the harvesters to leave enough grapes on the vine for the needy among the people; he compares himself to a vintner who finds Israel as pleasing as "grapes in the desert."

Just when you think you have plenty of ingredients for a biblical fruit salad, apples show up, too. Solomon compares his lover's breath to the fragrance of apples. And who knew that the phrase "the apple of my eye" comes from the Bible, which describes God's delight and devotion to his people as well as our delight and devotion to God's instruction.

As I learned more about fruit in the Bible, it quickly became clear that I had to narrow my search. I decided to focus on one of the most prominent fruits of the Bible and one I wanted to know more about: figs.

That's when I noticed that after the Tree of Knowledge of Good and Evil and the Tree of Life, the Bible mentions a fruit tree. While Scripture never specifies the kind of illicit fruit consumed by Adam and Eve, some argue that it was the fig. With their lush, appetizing exterior, figs appear "more pleasant to the eyes" than apples, and we know the fig tree stood nearby since its leaves provided the first covering of sin and shame. This biblical fruit seemed ripe for the picking.

IF YOU'VE NEVER BEEN TO A FIG FARM

My smartphone contact list isn't exactly filled with fig farmers, so I employed the same method I used to find my Israeli tour guide, Ido. I asked everyone I encountered if they knew someone who grew figs, trusting that God would again make a divine connection. Soon I boarded a plane to Madera, California.

When I arrive at the farm's main offices, I meet Kevin, who I sense would rather be walking his fields than stuck in a room full of people. With his windblown hair and sun-soaked face, you may assume he spends his days catching waves, not as one of the world's foremost fig experts.

The gravel road rumbles and kicks up a dust cloud behind Kevin's truck as we turn into the orchard. The truck grinds to a halt in the middle of the acreage. To my knowledge, I have never seen a fig tree before, or if I have, I didn't realize it. The lush trees have wide leaves that canopy the grayish branches until they all but disappear. Kevin says that if the trees remain unpruned for a few winters, even their trunks will vanish behind the lush leaves.

I never expected such tiny fruit to emerge from such mighty trees.

From a distance, the fig tree appears fruitless; only when we draw closer does the fruit appear. This first harvest, also known as the *breva* crop, is beginning to ripen into a deep magenta. Kevin scoops up a fig that's fallen to the ground, pinches off the stem, and offers me a taste. The sweetness explodes in my mouth like syrup. Layers of berry jam notes unfold among the gentle crunch of seeds. The inner flesh appears rose and amber, like the insides of an overripe watermelon. I'd heard the finest pastry chefs' most innovative desserts don't stand a chance against a perfectly ripe fig. Now I understand why. Not only does the fruit taste scrumptious, but each fig contains more potassium than a banana, more fiber than a prune, and more calcium than a glass of milk.

Table Discovery: Ready to pick out fresh figs? The perfect-looking figs in the grocery store are not the best-tasting. Look for the fresh figs that have a wrinkle known as a "growth crack" or a white line down the side. The fig will appear like it's just begun to dehydrate naturally. That's when they're most delicious. Snap off the stem and eat whole—including the skin.

Kevin explains that dried figs are more well-known because the window to sell a ripe fig is so narrow. Once plucked from the tree, a fresh fig has only an eight- to fourteen-day window to be enjoyed. Many grocery stores refuse to sell ripe figs because of their high perishability.

Sweat beads on my forehead, and Kevin leads me beneath the shade of a taller tree. The temperature drops a dozen degrees. An insect buzzes near my head and I remember reading that figs need wasps to pollinate, but Kevin says that's only for select breeds of fig trees—not his. I can tell I'm not the first to ask him that question. He explains that his self-pollinate, then ripen in similar fashion to other fig trees.

I look up the tree's spiraling interior where fruit lines the branches like Christmas lights. Those closest to the trunk ripen first. Figs grow up the branch of last year's growth, he explains, and don't ripen all at once like other fruit. They ripen toward the tip of the branches last.

"These ones are ready to pick," he says, pointing to two purplish orbs within arm's reach. The next two figs will ripen several days later, the next pair a week later. This continues for three weeks until all the figs ripen for the first harvest.

Because these are the first figs of the season, they're always the most anticipated, Kevin explains with a sparkle in his eyes. The next harvest will be sweeter and larger, but the *breva* crop is beloved among fig aficionados because it's a sign that winter is over and figs will add sweetness to tables for months to come. This *breva* crop is what Hosea compares Israel to when he is "seeing the early fruit on the fig tree."

Unlike most fruit trees, figs are multi-cropping, which means they are harvested numerous times each year. In a few months, a second harvest begins where the *breva* crop stops on the branch. Once again, the figs will ripen from the bottom of this year's new growth, in pairs or trios. While Kevin's current fig farms produce only two crops per year, some of the fig trees in ancient Israel were known to produce three per year, meaning they produced fruit nearly year-round.

The Hebrew word for harvesting figs, *oreh*, means "light of dawn."

Because ripe figs spoil quickly, farmers must wake early daily to see if the next handful is harvestable. Those who harvest figs must live expectantly.

Among religious Jews, sitting under a fig tree symbolizes devout study of the Torah. Just as the figs ripen slowly on the tree, so Scripture ripens with new discoveries as we study. The more one observes, the more one discovers.

As we move from tree to tree, Kevin monitors my progress and points out the best fruit to pick. My mind wanders to two men who are likewise found beneath the leaves of fig trees. The Gospel of John describes Nathanael enjoying this particular tree's shade when he learns of Jesus. And later, a man named Zacchaeus catches a glimpse of Jesus after climbing a sycamore-fig. The Hebrew name for sycamore-fig is *shikma,* a word whose root means "rehabilitate," and  Just as the figs ripen slowly on the tree, so Scripture ripens with new discoveries as we study.

that's exactly what happens in this story. Zacchaeus climbs down from his safe observation post in the rehabilitation tree and into a whole new life, healed by Jesus and his love.

Suddenly a giant plume of dust appears in the distance, and Kevin urges me back into the vehicle. The farm uses huge wind machines with airplane propellers to shake the thirty-foot-tall trees so the ripe figs fall to the ground. Then pickers rake the figs between rows to be sun-dried and processed.

"Let's take you to where we handpick figs," he suggests.

A few miles down the road, we enter a fig grove so heavily pruned the trees grow no more than ten feet tall. Their short stature allows the workers to handpick the fruit. The harvesters wear protective clothing from head to toe despite the triple-digit temperature. The layers and gloves safeguard pickers from the caustic, milky sap known as *ficin* as well as the irritating hairs found on the outside of fig leaves. I watch as the harvesters gather fresh figs in white buckets. When it's time for lunch, the workers take breaks under the cool shade of the trees.

Kevin hands me a pair of gloves and two clear plastic clamshell containers and invites me to fill them up. Recognizing a ripe fig requires a skill I don't have. Kevin advises me to pick only those that have the darkest color, signifying they're the ripest.

As he points me to the best ones, I remember that Jesus doesn't just call followers from fig trees, but he teaches parables about them, too. One of his stories centers around a fig tree planted in a vineyard. The owner in the story complains that he's hunted for sweet fruit on this particular fig tree for three years, but nothing ever grows. In frustration, he suggests tossing out the tree and using the precious real estate to plant something more fruitful. The caretaker asks for another year to fertilize and care for the tree. If the tree still doesn't produce, then it will be cut down.

Table Discovery: Ready to explore fig varieties? If you see fresh figs in your local grocery and don't find a label, ask the staff in the produce department about the type. You may be tasting black missions, brown turkeys, sierras, or kadotas. Kevin's favorite is the tiger fig, with its green and yellow stripes. If you see more than one variety available, try them all and share with friends.

Many who heard this teaching were acquainted with the care and maintenance of fig trees. The trees require fertilizer and pruning. The shoots that pop up from the roots like periscopes must be trimmed. If allowed to grow wild, they suck energy from the tree, impeding its ability to produce fruit. In addition, many fig varieties don't grow fruit until their fourth year. Listeners to Jesus's story recognize the caretaker's response as one of wisdom and grace. If the tree is chopped down, though it would eventually sprout new life, it will take many more years to bear fruit.

Instructing the disciples to pay attention to the times, Jesus turns to the fig again: "Now learn the lesson from the fig tree: as soon as its twigs get tender and its leaves come out, you know that summer is near."

I knew that most fruit trees blossom before the fruit buds. Like a pomegranate's bright orange flowers or an apple's pinkish blooms, the flowers indicate that fruit is coming. As we're picking fruit, Kevin mentions that a fig is the flower turned in on itself; therefore, the flowers of figs are never visible. The most noticeable sign of coming figs is that the branches lose their rigidity and become more pliable.

Then, he notes that figs themselves appear monochromatic. They change color only in the few days they ripen. If a person doesn't pay attention and study the ripening of figs, the harvest can be missed. No wonder Jesus uses figs as a metaphor to look closely and pay attention for his return and everyday presence.

A peek at the clock reveals my time on the farm has snuck by like a thief, and I race to catch my flight. Before I leave, Kevin gives me a bag to carry my figs home. Now I can't wait to gather my fruit-picking friends and share the succulent figs as well as what I'm discovering.

WHEN EXPECTATIONS SHAPE YOUR PERCEPTIONS

My time with the fig farmer changed the way I read the almost six dozen mentions of figs in the Bible. As I reflected on the experience, I realized the fig was nothing I had expected. Up until my time with Kevin, I had always thought fig trees were like the other fruit trees I enjoyed while harvesting the neighborhood—blossoming in spring, growing during the early summer, and ripening just before fall.

Whenever Jesus says, "Look at the fig tree," he is challenging our notions of attentiveness and expectations.

The figs can easily be missed. Instead of simply noticing showy blossoms, we must actually feel the branches to test their pliability. Then we must closely inspect them to detect the presence of developing fruit. We have to be close to the tree and engaged with its growth to reap the sweetest of harvests.

But there's a catch: Have you ever noticed that when you expect one thing, your attentiveness dulls to everything else?

Psychologists call this "change blindness," a term describing our tendency to miss shifts in our immediate visual environment. We assume that if something dramatic changes right before our eyes, we will, of course, recognize the shift. But actually, it's impossible for the human mind to fully process and be aware of every visual detail at all times. Sometimes large changes in scenes go unnoticed either because of our preconceived notions or our focus on some other detail—so much so that we can miss them altogether. In one experiment, a person came alongside a pedestrian and struck up a conversation. During an intentional distraction, a different experimenter replaced the initial one. Only half of the pedestrians noticed they were now talking to a different person.

Though we're tempted to tell ourselves *we* would notice the difference, these kinds of changes slip by us in films every day. Have you ever noticed in *Star Wars: The Empire Strikes Back*, Han Solo's jacket disappears and then reappears as he says good-bye to Princess Leia? And did you see the white cars tootling through the background of the medieval Scottish countryside during the epic "ancient" battle scenes in *Braveheart?*

Our expectations shape our perceptions.

And not just in movies. This happens in our ordinary daily lives. We can become so focused on a desired outcome, like landing the promotion or raise, that we become less attentive to everyone and everything else around us. Before we know it, we're missing birthdays, arriving late to dinner with friends, and skipping sleep. Or perhaps we're so focused on the ways our spouse or best friend isn't meeting our needs that we miss all the opportunities for connection.

This kind of change blindness happens to the religious leaders who encounter Jesus. The long-awaited Messiah has spent three years walking among them. He restores people such as Zacchaeus, heals those born blind, fulfills prophecy right and left; yet many people miss the cultivating, nurturing, life-giving work of the Savior because he isn't who they expected a Messiah to be.

Sometimes we have the same problem: we miss the *breva* crop because we are looking for flamboyant blossoms. Or we focus too much on the disappearance of the first crop and forget a larger sweeter crop is coming. If we aren't on the lookout, we could easily miss our harvest. We become so laser-focused on one desired outcome, we become blind to the many ways God is working all around us.

In the Gospel of Mark, Jesus's final miracle is the withering of a fig tree. Jesus leaves Bethany, a place that means "house of the fig," and heads toward the temple in Jerusalem. On the way he eyes a fig tree without fruit, only leaves, out of season, and says, "May no one ever eat fruit from you again."

Those words can be misconstrued as tree cruelty at first glance. Why would Jesus say this?

Turns out that on multiple occasions in the Old Testament, when the prophets paint an image of a satisfying life with God, a close relationship with him, they describe people living under their own fig tree. The contentment and delight symbolized by such a scene are multilayered. The fig tree alludes to God's ongoing provision by way of its slow ripening and multiple crops. The fig leaves speak of God's tender care as some of the coolest shade to be found in Israel. The fruit speaks of God's sweetness through its delicious, nourishing sustenance.

Yet the fig tree Jesus sees is fruitless, so he proclaims this is now the permanent status of the tree. Notice that Jesus does this on the way to the temple where, upon arrival, he flips the merchandise tables and skedaddles the salespeople. The next day, Peter observes that the fig tree has withered.

In the proclamation over the fruitless fig tree and cleansing the temple, Jesus performs back-to-back symbolic acts. Like a fig tree with barren branches, the religious people have buildings but no spiritual vitality. When Jesus says, "May no one ever eat fruit from you again!" he speaks of the hypocrisy, legalism, and robbery teeming within their hearts.

Just as the fig tree is out of season, so too the season of the temple has passed. This will no longer be the place where the ritual system of forgiveness takes place. A new season has arrived with Christ the ultimate sacrifice, the ultimate authority, the ultimate temple. Jesus destroys the fig tree, much like he "tears down" the temple, so followers can see him more clearly and reorient their expectations toward true satisfaction in him.

Sometimes we're tempted to find that satisfaction somewhere, anywhere, other than in Christ. When we do, we find ourselves disillusioned, disappointed, and, worse, the fruit of the Spirit doesn't mature in us. Our accomplishment-driven society would have us assess our worth, the yield of our lives, with what wins the most accolades—landing the promotion, earning the higher degree, launching a successful venture, completing the marathon, retiring early. Yet personal or professional feats lead only to fleeting satisfaction. Like the image of people living contentedly under their own fig trees, our deepest hungers find their ultimate satisfaction when abiding in Christ.

HOW TO LIVE A LIFE WORTH SAVORING

Before I traveled to the farm, I read that one fig tree can produce 10,000 figs a year. That seemed like an enormous, unrealistic quantity. Ten thousand figs a year from one tree didn't seem possible, but who was I to say?

So, as you can imagine, it was an important question for Kevin.

"Maybe a wild fig—" Kevin said, "—but my trees produce 50,000 to 75,000."

My mouth fell agape. What if *that* is the image of fruitfulness God has for us?

Spiritual fruit is the result of being rooted in relationship with Christ. Any fruit—including love, joy, peace, patience, kindness, goodness, faithfulness, gentleness, and self-control—provides evidence of the work of the Holy Spirit. As we ground ourselves in God, he plants and weeds, nourishes and fertilizes, prunes and harvests. The yield of our fruitfulness are the qualities that make us look more like him.

Not only do figs uncover a need for close observation and reliance on God in surprising ways, I was also learning more than ever before about fruitfulness.

When I decided to be intentional about observing God's bounty, I started to notice fruitfulness everywhere, not just on the fig farm. One particular day I passed by a tree so bursting with nectarines, the fruit swept the ground. I realized that it's easy to trust God when the fruit of our lives abounds and appears easy to recognize, as on that nectarine tree.

In our most abundant moments, we live our lives like "the stars in heaven and the lilies in the field, perfectly, simply, and unaffectedly." These are the times when our branches are bowing low and our baskets are bountiful, and we feel satisfied.

But not all seasons or harvests burst with abundance. Sometimes, like the fig, we enter a difficult season. A spouse becomes emotionally unavailable, the adult child never calls, the boss refuses to say thank you. We lose a house or a business or our health or our identity and feel like we have nothing left to offer. We become change-blind to God's nourishing presence. If we're only looking for the bright blossoms, the big harvest, the banner season, then we'll miss so much of the work God is doing each and every day, in each and every season—even the difficult ones.

God isn't waiting for one particular season in the distant future to yield fruitfulness in our lives. He's working throughout every season and every harvesting cycle.

Sometimes we may grow frustrated when the fruit in our lives doesn't appear as spectacular or sweet as last season's. Perhaps that's because we are growing a *breva* crop in this new area of life. Maybe the spark I saw in Kevin's eyes when he talked about the first crop provided a glimmer of celebration that God has for us in our *breva* fruitfulness, whenever we find ourselves in a new age, stage, or location.

Sooner or later we'll all be tempted to believe that our best days are behind us. We'll measure ourselves more by what we can no longer do than by what we still can. We'll feel washed up and washed out. But the fig tree challenges this expectation, too. One of the beauties of the fig is that, once planted, the tree will continue to produce fruit for eighty to a hundred years. That's Christ's vision for us: that we will continue to yield the fruit of Christlikeness and find our satisfaction in him long after gray hairs sprout and crow's feet nestle near our eyes.

And when we see Jesus face-to-face, we will continue to bear an abundant crop with each harvest better than the last. God is infinite, and so we will never stop discovering new aspects of his marvelous character and we will never stop growing in our praise and adoration and joy in him.

Until then, we must start to think differently about the fruitfulness of our daily lives. God invites us to find our satisfaction in him, in the fruit he's yielding in us week after week, season after season, in quantities we never thought possible and in layers of jammy flavors we've never known before.

AROUND THE TABLE

What if we learned to celebrate the fruit in each other's lives? Living expectant that God is budding new life for one another? Noticing the fruit that's ever maturing in each other? Seeing the good work that God is growing in us?

Gather your family or a group of friends around the table. Take turns highlighting the fruit each person recognizes in each other's life. Consider each fruit of the Spirit—love, joy, peace, patience, kindness, goodness, faithfulness, gentleness, and self-control—and how that fruit is perhaps becoming evident as the person deepens their friendships, leads others well, embraces neighbors and strangers, or demonstrates a healthy work-life balance. Parents can think about the ways God is at work in their kids now and pray a blessing for a lifetime of fruitfulness over each child.

CHRISTY'S ROASTED FIGS AND BRUSSELS SPROUTS

This delicious roasted vegetable dish will be great as a side or an entire meal.

PREP: 15 minutes   **COOK:** 35 minutes   **COOL:** 5 minutes

2 cups of Brussels sprouts, trimmed and halved
1 small sweet onion, sliced
8 figs, halved
1 1/2 tablespoons olive oil
leaves from 6 sprigs of thyme
salt and pepper to taste
1 tablespoon aged balsamic vinegar

DIRECTIONS

1. Preheat oven to 400 degrees F.
2. Toss the Brussels sprouts, onion, and figs with the olive oil and place on a baking sheet lined with parchment paper. Sprinkle with thyme leaves, salt, and pepper.
3. Roast for about 30–35 minutes, turning the Brussels sprouts at least once to evenly roast.
4. Once the Brussels sprouts and onions caramelize and the figs appear slightly shriveled, remove from the oven and coat with the aged balsamic vinegar.

Serves 2–3.

CAROLYN'S SALTED CARAMEL WITH FIG SAUCE

This salted caramel sauce will become a family favorite and makes a great gift.

PREP: 20 minutes,   **COOK:** 20 minutes   **COOL:** 10 minutes plus 24–36 hours
of refrigeration

2 cups sugar
4 tablespoons unsalted butter
1 cup cream
1 teaspoon vanilla (or 1 vanilla bean)
1 tablespoon sea salt (or more, to taste)
2 tablespoons fig compote or jam
1 carton of vanilla ice cream

DIRECTIONS

1. Pour sugar into large pot with a heavy bottom and tall sides. Spread evenly across the bottom.
2. Heat the sugar over medium for 8–10 minutes. The sugar will slowly heat and melt around the edges. To prevent sugar crystals from forming, do not stir. If a spot starts to bubble, carefully pick up the pot and swirl. If sugar starts to smoke, turn down the heat.
3. Heat the cream and vanilla in the microwave for 1 minute until hot, but not boiling.

4. As the sugar starts to melt, keep swirling so it melts more evenly. Continue to let the sugar melt, swirling occasionally, until it darkens to a light caramel color. When sugar starts to simmer and looks like it has melted, stir lightly with a silicone spatula to ensure that all sugar is dissolved.

5. When the caramel has reached a rich golden tone, add the butter. Keep a careful eye on the sugar and don't let it darken too much. It can burn in a matter of seconds. You'll know it's ready when it starts to smell like caramel and is a dark amber color. Stir until it is melted.

6. Heat the fig compote or jam in microwave 1 minute or until melted.

7. Remove the sugar from heat and add the fig, cream, vanilla, and salt. If you'd like a super smooth caramel, strain through a fine metal sieve.

8. Pour caramel into a heatproof jar. Allow it to cool a few minutes before using.

9. Serve over ice cream, your favorite dessert, or as a dip for apples and bananas. Enjoy for your meal or share as a gift.

Makes 1–1/2 cups of sauce.

LAURI AND LEAH'S CHOCOLATE
POMEGRANATE DROPS

When Lauri first served these chocolate drop cookies, the sweet pop of juicy pomegranates and lush chocolate made me a lifelong fan. I hope you receive the same rave reviews from those you share them with—including your gluten-free friends.

PREP: 10 minutes   **COOK:** 3 minutes   **COOL:** 45 minutes

2 pomegranates
12 oz. bag of semi-sweet chocolate chips

DIRECTIONS

1. Remove the juicy seeds from the pomegranates or buy them pre-removed. If you're removing the pulpy seeds (which resemble grains of corn), use a sharp knife to score the outside skin of the pomegranate. Fill a medium-sized mixing bowl with water and break the pomegranate open under the water. This prevents the juice from spraying and the seeds will sink to the bottom, separating from the pulp, which will float to the top. Rinse and strain the pulpy seeds.
2. Dry the outside of the juicy seeds completely.
3. Melt chocolate chips either on the stove or in a microwave-safe dish. If you're using the microwave, I recommend heating half of the bag at a time and stirring frequently until completely melted.

4. Set aside a small portion of the seeds for garnishing at the end. Gently mix the remaining seeds in with the melted chocolate. Some people prefer more chocolate or more pomegranates, so you can play with the proportions.
5. Spoon tablespoonfuls of the chocolate-pomegranate mixture onto a baking sheet that has been covered in wax paper or parchment. Garnish each clump with a few non-chocolatey pomegranate seeds for presentation. Chill in the fridge about 30–45 minutes until they harden.

Makes 15–20 drops.

A Loaf of Bread Just Out of the Oven

TASTE AND SEE GOD'S COMMUNITY

I peer through the oven's glass window, coated with splatters from past meals, to assess the bread baking inside. More than anything, I *don't* want the bread to rise.

I wish I knew more about the finicky nature of this particular range, but this isn't my stove. This isn't even my kitchen. I've traveled from Utah to Connecticut to try my hand at unleavened bread.

When I launched my baking expedition to explore bread in the Bible, I looked for local bakers to deepen my understanding of bread and its rich imagery throughout Scripture. One chef led to another, and soon I scoured a variety of resources on how this particular food rose to prominence throughout history.

Somewhere along the way, I stumbled on a resource by Andrew McGowan, the dean of Berkeley Divinity School at Yale University and knew he would be the very best guide. He's both an Episcopal priest and an expert on ancient bread making. Jackpot!

With Ido-inspired chutzpah, I invited myself to visit the prestigious Ivy League campus and spend an afternoon baking in his kitchen. He graciously accepted my request, and before I knew it, I found myself at Yale.

At first glance, Andrew looks like a fine-art auctioneer at Christie's. Untamed salt-and-pepper hair grazes his shoulders. Mod glasses frame his wise owl-like eyes. Yet it's the puff of flour on his tie that's impossible to ignore. I have a suspicion that he isn't a typical seminary professor, and my hunch is confirmed when he leads me into the kitchen of his campus home.

Instead of cabinets, cherry-red shelves line the pale walls. They are stocked with my all-time favorite brand of spices. A whimsical white tea kettle with black polka dots rests atop the stove. Unlike my unkempt kitchen, Andrew's appears tidy with every item assigned to its proper place.

The centerpiece of the kitchen is an oversized wooden countertop designed for baking with a lower-set edge and a plastic barrier to prevent runaway flour. I follow Andrew to his personal treasure vault: a pantry stuffed with eclectic flours from around the world.

"I collect flour like some collect power tools," he says with a gusty laugh.

Andrew scans the labyrinth of ground grains to select the ingredients for today's culinary adventure. He gathers several flours and cradles them in his arms like infants. Then we return to the kitchen and I pull up a stool to his baking table.

"We're going to make authentic matzo like the Israelites ate,"

Andrew announces. "From the start to out-of-the-oven, we have only eighteen minutes."

HOW TO AVOID THE LEAVEN OF THE PHARISEES (HINT: YOU CAN'T)

I know unleavened bread is a Jewish staple that commemorates the night when God instructs the Israelites to flee Egypt at lightning speed. It's said that they left in such a hurry that they could not wait for bread dough to rise. But why only eighteen minutes?

Andrew explains that a basic mixture of water and flour rises, or leavens, on its own with enough time.

water + flour + time = leavened bread

Centuries ago, a pair of rabbis debated how long a Jewish baker could work with dough before it bubbles and leavens. In the famous exchange, one rabbi suggested eighteen minutes and the other, twenty-four minutes. Because they loved the law of God, the rabbis believed the best way to help people observe the law was to not exceed the regulation's basic requirement. If you don't want to cross a line, the reasoning goes, then stay away from it. As a result, if rabbis had a dispute between two guidelines, the stricter was always favored. To uphold their love for the law and make certain no lines were crossed, the rabbis agreed on the shorter time for unleavened bread.

This explains what I experienced while in Israel. Leading up to Passover, the removal of leaven creates a physical spring-cleaning and represents a deeper spiritual one. Jewish households, and restaurateurs like Ido, don't focus on the yeast; they focus on the flour, which contains the capacity to become leaven.

In search of hidden *hametz*, the Hebrew word for leaven, people pull stoves from the walls, tear apart pantries, and scour the entire house to remove every last granule of flour. While more liberal Jews give their leavened food to Gentiles to store, the most conservative burn it.

One day while driving along the Galilee, I detected smoke rising from a nearby beach. I whipped the car around, daydreaming that maybe I'd see Jesus and the disciples enjoying breakfast. Instead, I discovered orthodox Jewish children standing around a fire pit burning their families' *hametz*.

In light of my experiences in Israel and Andrew's insights, I realized I'd either missed or misunderstood biblical references to leaven my entire life.

Wherever a passage refers to leaven or yeast, I interpreted the mention with modern ears. I'd imagine the baker reaching for an outside ingredient like a packet of Fleishmann's rapid-rise to make dough bubble. Alas, commercial yeast wasn't even invented until 1868.

Instead, the ancient Israelites used the same ingredients people work with today to make sourdough bread: water, flour, and time (and sometimes a starter ball of dough from a previous baking that is comprised of—you guessed it—water, flour, and time).

This illuminates Jesus's warning to beware the yeast of the Pharisees and Sadducees. This isn't a cautionary advisement against an outside contaminant. Rather, Jesus says, the same leaven that's in them is already in you. Our real enemy isn't what we see in others but what rises within us.

The same leaven that's in them is already in you.

The judgmental nature, the critical eye, the insidious pride we notice in others, wait to rise up in us too.

Maybe you've felt the leaven bubbling in your heart.

One particular person in my life causes me to sour. I am annoyed by her religiosity, by her black-and-white rigidity, by her constant assessments that no one can live up to. When she asked that a girl who uses a wheelchair be removed from her daughter's play-group because she slowed her child down, I wanted to throw a desk through the window. And by desk, I mean her.

Just like that, I realize that what's rising in her heart is identical to what's in mine.

If I allow my annoyance to rise, my leaven will push me away from her and her friends. The swelling in me can disrupt our entire community. No matter how justified we feel, there's no space for judgment in our hearts. It rises up and makes us cynical and angry toward others until we're tiptoeing around the very people we're meant to engage and embrace.

Of course, Jesus tells us to beware of the *hametz*. The only antidote to the leaven of sin is Christ's work in us. We must invite Christ to pull us away from our judgments, tear open our intentions, and scour our hearts. When we do this, we are able to live in a closer relationship with God and others.

WHEN EIGHTEEN MINUTES IS BARELY ENOUGH TIME

Retrieving a red stoneware Le Creuset bowl from the shelf and a matching plastic mat, Andrew pours a combination of barley and emmer flour. I'd never heard of emmer before. The grain is translated as "spelt" in the Bible and also known as *farro*.

To this day, no one knows which flours the Israelites used the night they fled Egypt, but Andrew makes an educated guess. He's chosen barley and emmer because of these grains' ability to tolerate poor soils and still produce high yields. These characteristics made them popular in the ancient world—especially among the poor.

As he bypasses the measuring cups and scales on the counter, Andrew explains that in antiquity cooks often lacked access to weights or measurements. Most ancient bakers learned to cook without them.

"For us, it's good to practice," he reminds.

I'm curious what we'll add to spice up the recipe. Sea salt? Garlic? Oil? Nothing at all, he advises, because this is the bread of necessity, the bread of affliction.

"Not even a pinch of salt?" I prod.

"You must remember when the Israelites escaped Egypt, they were not having a wonderful time," he explains. "The matzo during Passover isn't celebratory but commemorative."

The oven dings at 490 degrees. Andrew sets eighteen minutes on a timer, then pours water into the mix. His agile fingers dance throughout the dough. He pauses to add a splash of water or a sprinkle of flour to achieve the right consistency. A baseball-sized portion emerges. He maneuvers the mound back and forth on the plastic kneading mat.

"You must practice," he says, nudging the dough my direction.

Kneading gives the bread its texture and stability. I repeat the same motions, but odd shapes, not at all lunar, emerge from my efforts.

Eleven minutes.

Andrew snatches a rolling pin from the drawer and pinches the dough into four pieces. He dusts the kneading sheet with flour, then rotates one piece of dough back and forth with the pin until a flat, tortilla-looking object emerges.

"You do the next one."

Seven minutes.

Sweat drips from my forehead as I roll the dough hard and fast. The shape looks suspiciously like Jabba the Hutt.

I scoop the form onto a parchment-lined pan.

Andrew hands me another lump of dough. I thought the "bread of affliction" was something you ate, not something you do.

Five minutes.

Now for the marks of affliction. Using a fork, we pierce the thin layer like a checkerboard. For a bread to be considered unleavened, none of the naturally occurring air pockets can measure more than an inch in diameter. Messianic Jews at Passover sometimes compare the indentations to the holes or stripes of Christ in his suffering and death.

Andrew slips the pans into the oven. Together, we watch the countdown. He pulls the unleavened bread out with three seconds to spare. We barely make it. I can't help but wonder if that's how God's people felt when they disappeared into the night.

BREAD'S PLACE AT THE TABLE

The flat, unleavened bread looks like an oversized round cracker. Unlike prepackaged matzo sold at the store, this right-out-of-the-oven bread has a soft, chewy consistency.

"Add this," he advises, smearing on a dollop of white goat butter. The bread takes on the flavor of fresh goat cheese. Nom, nom.

I'm chewing on a slice of history. When humans transitioned from being hunter-gatherers toward farming, bread made its first major advancement in the Fertile Crescent of the modern Middle East. Genesis alludes to this shift when Jabal's descendants live in tents and raise livestock, while his brother, Tubal-Cain, forges all kinds of tools from bronze and iron. Grains flourished with the invention of the plow.

Portions of the harvests were mushed into porridge. Others were baked. Beans and other legumes and anything forage-able that offered the slightest nutrition were added to the dough. Ancient loaves were dense, dry, and heavy. Most contained so many impurities, including small rocks, they would be deemed a dental hazard and inedible today. Yet most of the world lived hungry, and any source of food was received as a gift.

From bread's earliest days, fluffy white rolls and loaves were always more desirable and enjoyed by the social elite. The peasantry relied on darker grain breads baked every few weeks or months. Some of these loaves became so stale, pieces had to be hacked apart and soaked in water before they could be consumed.

Throughout history, wars were fought and empires overthrown over lack of access to this basic food. The rising cost of bread played a key role in the start of the French Revolution as well as the more recent Arab Spring uprisings.

Only recently have innovations led to the ability to create inexpensive, mass-produced bread, with its uniform shape, bright white appearance, spongy texture, low cost, and even slices. Ironically, now the pendulum swings in more affluent countries back to the darker, chewier, artisanal whole wheat breads. Even in bread, we crave what's harder to obtain.

In some developed countries today, bread creates a different kind of rift. The warm loaves that once drew families together have now become a source of division with the recent surge in food allergies and calorie counting.

I know I'm not the only one who struggles with allergies or intolerances to certain kinds of grains. It's estimated that 1 percent of Americans have celiac disease, an autoimmune disease requiring a strict gluten-free diet, and eighteen million Americans have non-celiac gluten intolerance. Some people simply feel better when they don't eat bread. Others eliminate bread from their diets to trim calories or embrace breadlessness as part of a low-carb lifestyle.

Avoiding bread is a privileged choice. To this day, much of earth's population derives the majority of its calories from baked grains. With an estimated 30 percent of human calories derived from bread, only the wealthiest people in the richest parts of the world can afford to stop eating it. If eliminated from our collective diet, two billion people would starve to death within months.

Table Discovery: God commands Ezekiel to use a combination of "wheat and barley, beans and lentils, millet and spelt" to make bread. If you'd like to experiment with new baking recipes, all of these flours can be ordered online. Leif and I have been enjoying experimenting with bean flours, which are gluten free.

The opportunity to skip bread was never an option in the ancient world. In Hebrew, the word for bread, *lechem*, is synonymous with "food." When God says to Adam, "By the sweat of your face, you will eat your bread," some translations read, "you will have food to eat." Even the "staff of bread," also described as the "staff of life," implies that bread is so essential that it makes it possible for a person to walk.

Indeed, if you follow the breadcrumbs through the Old Testament, you'll find them appearing at pivotal moments. Remember the poor baker for whom Joseph delivers nightmarish news. And Sarah, who bakes for a holy trio, then learns a baby is on the way. Jacob adds a slice to the meat stew when he convinces Esau to sell his birthright, and Elijah survives on the bread of ravens. Then there's Gideon, who gains confidence from a dream about bread; meanwhile, Boaz and Ruth, share an appetizer involving—you guessed it—bread.

Who can forget that incredible moment when God sprinkles the desert with "manna," a bread so mysterious you'll never find it on a grocery shelf? Raised on the bread of Egypt, the people of God view the wafers from heaven with suspicion and ask, *"Manna?"* which, in Hebrew, means "What is this?" But the question runs much deeper than *What's this newfangled dish on God's menu?*

The Israelites have known only enslavement for generations. The honeyed bread of heaven contrasts with the stale bread of their sweaty toil in Egypt. Now God promises to feed his children for free and give them an entire day of rest each week. The offer seems too ridiculous, too foreign, too unbelievable. In this context, *What is this?* takes on new meaning.

The only life the people of God have experienced is slavery, exploitation, and hoarding. Manna upends all they've ever known.

In Egypt, Pharaoh demands bread.

In the wilderness, God dispenses bread.

In Egypt, the Israelites endure hard labor to survive.

In the wilderness, the Israelites gather with ease.

In Egypt, those who lord it over the Israelites do so for their own profit and gain.

In the wilderness, the Lord provides for his people's freedom and abundance.

In Egypt, bread symbolizes human power.

In the wilderness, bread symbolizes God's divine power.

Even the delivery mechanism of the sweet bread trumpets a new day has come for the Israelites. In Egypt, God declares, "I will rain down the worst hail that has ever occurred in Egypt from the day it was founded until now." In the wilderness, God showers bountiful, delicious provision.

God invites the entire community to rise and shine, to taste and see his goodness together. "In the evening you will know that it was the LORD who brought you out of Egypt, and in the morning, you will see the glory [or presence] of the LORD."

For those brutalized under Egyptian rule, the free lunch seems too good to be true. It takes forty years in the wilderness to recognize how much love, grace, and freedom God kneads into every morsel.

With so many mentions of bread, I know I'm just beginning.

WHAT GOD WHISPERS THROUGH BREAD

I wipe a schmear of goat butter from my bottom lip.

"One more thing . . . working on . . . must try," Andrew mutters, pulling a tray from a low hidden shelf.

The pan contains what appear to be four large, unbaked molasses cookies with sea salt. But they aren't cookies at all. The round, flattish loaves are bread—half barley, half emmer flour, seasoned with cumin—still popular in Morocco today. The oven must cool to 450 degrees before they can bake.

While waiting, Andrew explains the communal nature of bread making.

In ancient Israel, the whole family shared the hard labor. The work began in a field, plowing the soil and planting last year's kernels. Together, the family tended the field and prayed away famine and pests, in hope the stalks would sprout, lengthen, and yield a bounty of food.

The family endured sunburn and sweat, aching muscles and strained backs, to harvest the grain with sickles. When the yield was at hand, the work had just begun. Then they must pound and winnow (blow air) through the grain to remove the outer husk. Those who couldn't afford access to a mill used their own mortar and pestle to grind their grain.

Since the harvest had to carry the family through an entire year, only a small scoop of the flour was mixed with water and kneaded in a bread trough, while the bulk of the flour was safely stored away. The dough was then taken to the oven—but not a family oven. Most families couldn't afford their own stove. Instead, they used a communal oven.

"With so many loaves in a single oven, how did the families tell them apart?" Andrew asks with a professorial tone.

I can't solve the riddle.

Andrew shows me an image of two ancient loaves from AD 79. After a nearby volcano buried Pompeii, the round masses were preserved to perfection inside an oven. Each loaf bears an insignia according to its baker. That's how families identified their baked goods.

What catches my attention are the pizza-slice-shaped cuts on the breads' surfaces, which allowed the loaves to be easily broken into portions, and explains why, wherever bread appears in the Bible, there's never a mention of a bread knife nearby. The pre-cuts allowed people to tear the bread with ease, hence the term "breaking bread."

Remember Jesus's flagship miracle of feeding five thousand people? Out of nowhere, a boy offers to donate his lunch—a child so unencumbered that he imagines his meager offering can make a difference. Andrew, Simon Peter's brother, raises the question, "Here is a boy with five small barley loaves and two small fish, but how far will they go among so many?"

Tucked into this question are carefully worded details. Notice that both the loaves and the fish are described as small. The numerals five and two are important because together they add up to the perfect number, seven, which symbolizes completeness or divine perfection throughout Scripture. But John adds a detail that none of the other Gospel writers add, and only a foodie would notice: the type of loaves.

Twice in the story, the bread is described as barley, the food of peasants.

Those loaves are likely marked by pocks from pebbles, stained with blackened ash from the oven, and embedded with charred grass. Jesus doesn't multiply fluffy white bread. In using this particular flat loaf, Jesus echoes the refrain his presence has been singing since his birth in the stable. Jesus aligns with the poor.

After the crowds are satiated, the disciples gather a dozen basket-fuls of "broken pieces." I always imagined the leftovers as crumbs. Yet they were more likely pre-scored portions of bread, which at the time were whole servings.

The boy gives the barley loaves, and they represent the hard work, sacrifice, and gifts of the entire family. Together, the boy's family has nurtured and invested in those grains. The communal act is inherent in the planting and cultivating and harvesting and kneading and baking and sacrificing.

This communal nature stands in stark contrast to how many of us live today. Often when we encounter bread today, it's a solo affair. We select a plastic-wrapped, perfectly shaped loaf from the shelf and race to the self-checkout or even place an online order that arrives at our door. All too often we eat in our cars and cubicles. More and more, we procure food alone and eat alone.

Yet this hasn't always been the way.

From the beginning, bread was shared around a table—a table of working together, a table of living together, a table of vulnerability, a table of sacrifice, a table of thanksgiving. God set this table for the Israelites in the wilderness so they remember their deliverance. Christ set this table for the disciples in the upper room so we remember his sacrifice.

With every morsel of manna, God whispers that we are never meant to go it alone.

With every morsel of communion, God whispers that we are never meant to go it alone.

Sometimes we must shake ourselves free from a world with lab-designed food and freewheeling individualistic spirituality and remember—from the field to the seed to the growth to the harvest to the grinding to the baking to the serving—the bread we eat is a communal act of God with us and us with each other.

Jesus reveals, "I am the bread of life," and calls us to pray, "Give us today our daily bread." Before his departure, Jesus instructs,

"Take and eat; this is my body." Jesus could have instituted any act in memory of him—the teaching of others, the washing of the feet, the removal of a betrayer. Yet he prescribes one act in remembrance: sip the wine as blood and chew the bread as body. Christ comes to earth in the presence of the Father and the Spirit. He doesn't come alone, and the bread he calls us to eat is not meant to be consumed alone. He invites us to partake in the fullness of the Father, Son, Spirit, and community of the saints.

We are created to live life around a table in the taking and breaking, giving and sharing, knowing and being known. Bread welcomes us into the community for which our souls were made.

Bread welcomes us into the community for which our souls were made.

Andrew pulls the Moroccan loaves from the oven. The cumin adds a hint of heat to the soft, hearty bread. Before I leave to catch my return train, Andrew slides a few loaves of the unleavened and flatbread in my bag. I'm grateful for the food, but even more, for the friendship.

THE EIGHTEEN-MINUTE LOAF CHALLENGE

One of my most regrettable moments in Israel involved our daily bread. Ido's family and staff and I shared many meals together. We grew close fast, and I transformed from newfound friend to long-lost cousin.

Every meal featured all the bread anyone could eat. The meals before Passover included enormous focaccia drizzled with olive oil and dotted with fresh garlic. Like mine, most people's eyes were bigger than their bellies. Long after the plates were cleared, huge slabs of the uneaten bread remained on the tables.

In a desire to help, I cleaned and tossed the leftovers for the first few days. Then I became curious, for it seemed as if the bread had been left purposely to linger on the tables.

"Because it's holy," Mama Vered explained. "We offer it to the poor, and if they do not take it, we feed the birds and fish, but we never throw bread away."

Gulp. How many times had I flippantly discarded bread—not just at their table but at ours?

Bread plays a sacred role in Jewish life. Every loaf contains an element of mystery and hallowedness. Each bite provides a reminder of the privilege of food, not to be taken for granted, and of the hope of blessing the bread in the messianic future.

Table Discovery:
Recognizing the importance of bread has caused me to discover creative ways to save or discard aging bread. I'm now likely to toss excess into the freezer and toast, bake into croutons, or feed to the squirrels and birds. And whenever I bake a loaf for a meal with guests, I try to bake a second to send home with them—including gluten free.

I make a commitment to never again waste bread even though it will require some culinary ingenuity, like using the leftovers to bake croutons or stuffing. These practices will make me more attentive to the food I buy. They will remind me to avoid waste and consider the poor, who don't have such luxurious excess. The heels or crusts aren't as easy to discard when you recognize the labor that goes into each loaf and those who don't have access. Breaking bread as a communal act doesn't just occur around our tables but long before the loaves land in our baskets.

When Jewish farmers plant the grains, the name of God rests on their lips, and when they harvest, syllables of gratitude rise from their lips. Even to this day, whenever bread is eaten, a special blessing is said:

"Barukh atah Adonai Elohaynu melekh ha-olam ha-motzi lechem min ha-aretz."

Blessed are you, Lord, our God, King of the universe, who brings forth bread from the earth.

My Jewish friends pray this each time they tear a loaf. After my times with Ido and Andrew, I suspect bread can play a more sacred role in all of our lives.

I wonder if I too can use bread to draw people together. I resolve to bake unleavened bread with others—in under eighteen minutes, of course. The barley and emmer flour soon arrive on my doorstep from an online store (although, harvesting grain in our rocky backyard may become a future endeavor. Sorry, neighbors!). I approach my first baking buddy, and even though Leif appears skeptical at first, he joins in the preparations.

Without the oversight of Andrew or his custom bread-kneading table, flour flies in all directions. The dough becomes rock hard, then a gooey mess. The pressure of eighteen minutes creates some stress.

But I am determined.

With more time and practice, Leif and I learn to maneuver at a faster pace. Our bread rises less and less. Most bakers would consider this a disaster, but for us, this marks a major accomplishment.

A week into our matzo-making adventure, my friend Jess accepts an invitation to cook together. She arrives with her spry wit and bounty of bread-baking insecurities, but with a nudge from Leif, we manage to pull the flat bread out with a second to spare. Then comes Heidi, who, with an ever-determined eye, slides the loaves from the oven with three minutes left. Then Troy, a minister at our church, with whom we miss the deadline, but our conversation is so rich, nobody minds.

I now recognize bread as communal, our oven as communal, our spiritual growth as communal.

Even with the time limit, baking causes us to slow down and experience something meaningful together. The people we invite into our kitchen help make our house a home. As we bake, we share our stories, our laughter, our lives. In the process we nourish each other in the ways of Christ. We partake of the life-giving generosity of heaven here on earth.

When God sends manna or Jesus says, "I'm the bread of life," he's saying, *I want to be the center of your table, the center of your relationships, the center of your community.* This is true whether you use whole grains or gluten-free flour. Our flat breads and fluffy rolls and artisanal loaves invite us to taste and see the mystery and sacredness of God. They invite us to refuel, to remember, and most important, to feast on spiritual bread together. To talk and really listen. To share each other's burdens. To give the gift of our presence. And that presence is the best thing since . . . well, you know!

When God sends manna or Jesus says, "I'm the bread of life," he's saying, *I want to be the center of your table, the center of your relationships, the center of your community.*

Jesus picks bread as a primary metaphor for himself. As the bread of life, Jesus, the One who saves and sustains us in the wilderness, the center of our fellowship, the One our lives depend on, says, "Whoever eats this bread will live forever."

That's the table Christ sets for every eater.

And if you don't yet have community in your life, remember that finding those people may not be as hard as you think. Perhaps it begins with some flour, some water, and eighteen minutes.

AROUND THE TABLE

Take the eighteen-minute bread challenge. Invite friends or family, neighbors or newcomers, to make matzo together. You can use emmer, barley, wheat, or gluten-free flours.

ANDREW'S 18-MINUTE MATZO

A delicious way to involve friends and newcomers into your kitchen and life.

PREP: 12 minutes **COOK:** 5 minutes **COOL:** optional

1 cup flour (wheat, barley, spelt or gluten-free flour)
1/3 cup water
parchment paper

OPTIONAL (AND LESS KOSHER) ADDITIONS:
1 tablespoon olive oil
1/2 teaspoon salt
melted chocolate chips
peanut butter
goat butter
your favorite cheeses

DIRECTIONS

1. Preheat oven to 450. Set timer to 18 minutes and start it when water is added to the dough.
2. Mix ingredients together and knead well but quickly. Add more flour if sticky, or water if the flour is not all incorporated.
3. Divide into 2–5 pieces as desired and roll out on lightly floured surface, as thin as practicable, turning often to prevent sticking.

4. Place on cookie sheet dusted with flour or covered with baking parchment and prick well with a fork.
5. Bake until crisp and beginning to brown, between 4 to 5 minutes. Remove from oven within the 18 minutes from-start-to-finish timeframe.

Serves 4.

———————

For a less kosher option, add oil and salt. If you want to add some sass, drizzle chocolate and peanut butter or add goat butter or cheese after baking. Or serve with an olive-fig tapenade included in the olive chapter's recipes.

Once you've completed your flat bread, I'd love to see what you bake and who you bake it with. Send your photos to hello@margaretfeinberg.com.

KHUBZ BELBOULA: ANDREW'S MOROCCAN BARLEY BREAD

This is a flavorful bread Andrew shared with me during my visit. It's delicious with a pat of butter and jam or to soak up your favorite main dish sauces.

PREP: 2 hours 30   **COOK:** 20 minutes **COOL:** none minutes

2 cups barley flour (available from some specialty stores and online)
2 cups all-purpose flour
2 teaspoons sugar
1/3 teaspoon salt
1 tablespoon cumin seeds
4 teaspoons dry yeast
2 tablespoons olive or vegetable oil
1–1/2 cups warm water, approx.
Optional: 1 tablespoon barley grits or semolina

DIRECTIONS

1. Toast the cumin seeds for 2–3 minutes in a heavy bottomed pan.
2. In a large bowl, combine the flours, sugar, salt, toasted cumin seeds, and yeast.
3. Add the oil and the water, mixing to make a dough.
4. Turn the dough out onto a floured surface, or into a stand mixer fitted with a dough hook.

Knead for 5 to 10 minutes, or until the dough is smooth and elastic.

5. Divide the dough into 4–6 portions as you prefer, then shape each portion into a smooth hemispherical mound. Brush each mound with a little water, then roll in grits/semolina (if desired), pressing gently to help the grits adhere to the dough. Transfer the loaves to a baking sheet. Cover the dough with a towel and let rest for 10 to 15 minutes.

6. Use the palm of your hand to flatten the dough into circles about 1/4"–1/2" thick. Cover again, and let rise for about two hours, until the dough springs back when pressed lightly with a finger. Preheat oven to 435 degrees F.

7. Score the top of the bread with a knife, or prick with a fork. Bake about 20 minutes—rotating the pan about halfway through the baking time—or until the loaves appear lightly colored and sound hollow when tapped. These loaves freeze well.

Makes 6 loaves.

WES'S SIMPLE SOURDOUGH STARTER & BREAD

STARTER

Making a sourdough starter is the first step in opening the door to all kinds of delicious, nutritious, and traditionally baked breads and pastries.

PREP: 5 minutes   **PROCESS:** 3–5 days **COOL:** none

1-quart Mason jar with lid
1 five-pound bag of your favorite flour (non-white is
    recommended and an organic sprouted whole wheat
    flour gives a rustic sourdough loaf flavor)
lukewarm water

CREATING THE STARTER

1. Mix ¼ cup flour and ¼ cup warm water in a Mason jar until it looks like a pancake mix. Based on your climate and altitude, you may need to add in a splash more water or flour.
2. Cover the container loosely and allow mixture to stand overnight at room temperature.
3. Repeat these steps and continue adding to the starter for the next four days. Between days two and three, your starter will begin to bubble. You should be able to see air pockets on the side of your Mason jar and "rivulets" or fine air bubbles on the top of your mixture by day five. If not, remove ½ cup of starter and continue the same steps for two more days.

The starter should have a tangy aroma that's not overpowering. The bubbling mixture is now ready to use for baking.

MAINTAINING THE STARTER

1. Store the starter in the refrigerator with lid. Once or twice a week remove $1/2$ cup of starter and add $1/4$ cup flour and $1/4$ cup warm water.
2. Over time, the starter may develop a brown liquid on top. Before you use the starter again, pour off the brown liquid and remove $1/4$ cup of starter. Discard both.
3. Make sure you feed your starter each day before baking to strengthen and revive the starter.
4. If you bake frequently and want to keep the starter going, you can add water and flour daily or even twice a day.
5. Always make sure to add equal parts warm water and flour. You don't have to stick to a $1/4$ cup. You can use as little as a tablespoon in equal amounts or as much as a cup of each.

SIMPLE SOURDOUGH BREAD

Now that you have a simple starter, let's make some sourdough. Before you begin, you need to know some differences between sourdough and traditional bread. Unlike traditional bread, sourdough needs to be prepared a day in advance. The dough won't double in size in an hour like some traditional breads. And there's a chance you won't be successful on your first (or second) try. But with tenacity and practice, you'll be making mouthwatering artisanal loaves in no time.

PREP: 1–3 days **COOK:** 45–60 minutes **COOL:** 30 minutes

1 cup sourdough starter (preferably fed 3 hours before)
3–4 cups flour
1 1/2 cups warm water
2 teaspoons salt
Optional: 1 tablespoon olive oil

DIRECTIONS

1. Mix bubbly sourdough starter with 1 1/2 cups flour and 1 cup water in a bowl and whisk until the dough looks like batter.
2. Add salt and remaining flour. When you can no longer whisk, use your hands. Rather than knead the dough, practice folding it. Simply take dough from one side, stretch it up, and fold it on top. Repeat for each side of the dough. Continue to add flour until the texture is sticky and still pourable.
3. Pour dough into loaf or pie pans until 1/3 full. Cover and allow to rest at room temperature for 8–12 hours or until double in size with a dome on the top.
4. Take a sharp serrated knife and slice the top of the loaves into a square.
5. Preheat oven to 350 degrees. Place your dough in the refrigerator to stabilize it while the oven preheats.
6. Bake bread for 45–60 minutes until the edges turn golden. If you prefer your bread browner, brush olive oil on top ten minutes before removing from oven. When you tap on the loaves, they should sound hollow.
7. Remove and allow to cool on wire racks.

Makes 2 loaves.

A Dash of Sea Salt

TASTE AND SEE GOD'S PURPOSE

If it weren't for salt, I might not exist.

My father manufactured surfboards in the 1960s as the surfing industry caught its first wave of widespread popularity. While delivering a shipment to Ron Jon Surf Shop, he noticed a young, attractive woman perusing the aisles. He approached her with an offer she couldn't refuse: if she agreed to meet for dinner, then she could purchase any of his surfboards at wholesale.

That very night they met at a local restaurant, and when her soup arrived, the woman salted her food without even tasting it. She became so enthralled in telling a story, she forgot the shaker in her hand.

My father's eyes widened as the white crystals continued to fall. The shaker slipped from her hand, and soup and salt splashed all over the table and the woman's shirt. The couple burst out laughing.

Something about my mother's joyous disposition captured my father's heart, and they recently celebrated their fiftieth wedding anniversary. My father says their first date prepared him for a lifetime with a woman who consumes salt in epic proportions.

Like my father, I often sat wide-eyed watching how much Mom salted food in our kitchen. But over time, my taste buds adjusted, and salt shifted from an optional addition to an absolute requirement for every meal. Now I'm the one people look at wide-eyed when I pile on the salt.

I may not be a salt sommelier, but when you visit our kitchen, you'll find my favorite member of the periodic table everywhere. Maldon salt, harvested from the cold waters of England, tastes delicious on roasted chicken. We rub gray French sea salt into beef. Near the stove rests a ramekin of pink Himalayan salt for everyday dishes. In our spice drawer, you'll find smoked salts, black salts, even Australian Murray River salt.

At fancy restaurants, I can become embarrassingly obsessive. If I'm planning to enjoy a steak, I BYOS (Bring Your Own Salt). On my plate, I build mini mountains of salt, then add freshly ground cracked pepper for each beefy bite. I'll even BYOS to Chick-fil-A and sprinkle it on every golden nugget of God's chicken.

Table Discovery:
I recommend replacing salt shakers with small dishes filled with salts from around the world. Each guest takes their pinch in the quantity and flavor they prefer.

Leif, concerned about my sodium levels, once urged me to visit a physician. After double-checking my blood pressure, the doctor explained that salt sensitivity varies. For some, blood pressure spikes with salt consumption. For others, it plummets or doesn't respond at all. To my relief, the doctor affirmed I can eat all the salt I want—dangerous words for a salt enthusiast like me. Now whenever someone raises an eyebrow around my heavy-handedness, I say with a wink, "Doctor's orders."

Even if your parents didn't bond over a salty first date, without salt you wouldn't exist either. The mineral presents itself in your saliva, your sweat, even your tears. Saline solution, a kind of salty water, has been used for wound irrigation and its antiseptic properties; it's where we get the idiom "rub salt in a wound." Salt, also known as sodium chloride, provides a crucial component of functioning cells. If you're taken to the hospital after a serious accident, the medical personnel will hook you up to an IV of saline while they determine what to do next. The mineral enables your nerves to transmit impulses and stimulates muscle fibers. If all the salt were drained from your body, your heart would cease to beat.

Table salt has become so common, accessible, and inexpensive today, we rarely pause to consider its value. If you visit a local restaurant and ask for salt, and the server whispers, "That'll cost extra," you'd probably wonder, "Huh?"

Yet for most of human history, salt has been a prized commodity. Early on, due to a lack of technology, salt proved notoriously difficult to harvest, and the difficulty of transportation inflated the costs. The ancient Egyptians ranked among the first to discover salt's culinary potential. They evaporated water from the Nile Delta, then applied the white granules to layers of meat and fish. In the process, they stumbled upon salt's ability to deter bacterial growth. The invention of curing allowed for year-round preservation of food in a world without refrigeration—a global game changer.

The popularity of the product bolstered trade and wealth among salt-producing empires. To overcome difficulties in transportation, the Romans built the Via Salaria, or "Salt Road," which became one of many historical trade routes to carry the precious cargo. The Romans viewed salt as vital to expanding their empire. When their soldiers went to war, they sweated profusely on the battlefield. The resulting salt deprivation led to confusion, seizures, even brain damage. To sustain their military, Rome began including salt, or *sal* in Latin, in their soldiers' pay. This is where we derive the word "salary."

Many of the culinary words we use today, including "salad," meaning vegetables seasoned with salt, and "sausage," meaning meat seasoned with salt, derive from the same Latin root.

Table Discovery:
Interested in new salts? Gray sea salt has a harsher flavor and works well with recipes that involve thyme, garlic, and cumin. Pair Himalayan salt with recipes that include rosemary, basil, and bay leaves.

After the fall of the Roman Empire, salt continued to play an important role in military enterprise. Napoleon discovered its importance when thousands of his troops died from wounds that failed to heal because of the soldiers' salt deficiencies. During the Civil War, a fierce battle ensued near Saltville, Virginia, because the Confederate army needed access to the salt reservoirs to sustain its troops.

Meanwhile, governments around the globe have imposed salt taxes that have enriched their coffers as well as dissolved their power. The French had to purchase their salt from royal depots during the reign of Louis XVI, and complaints about the cost of salt (along with bread) helped fuel the French Revolution. As recently as 1930, Mahatma Gandhi led a two-hundred-mile pilgrimage to collect untaxed salt for the poor of India.

I had no idea that something we're told to cut back on today played such an important role in history. Luckily, Leif and I now live in the perfect place for a salty adventure.

WHEN YOU'RE CAUGHT BETWEEN A ROCK AND A HARD PLACE

Utah is a sodium lover's dreamscape. Salt comes from evaporated dead seas or living ones, and you'll find a variety of such geological wonders throughout the state. The most famous, the Great

Salt Lake, sits less than an hour's drive from our home. Utah even named its capital city after this body of water. But don't mistakenly think you can bring your own shaker to fill up and take home from its shoreline. The salt taken from the lake isn't FDA-approved for human consumption.

The state also boasts the Bonneville Salt Flats, a vast area that feels like the surface of the moon with thirty thousand acres of white expanse. An adorable girl donning a canary-yellow dress appears on the side of the Morton's Salt plant located there. Most don't realize that Morton's salt is distinctly a modern product. The processed salt contains additional ingredients including calcium silicate for anticaking, dextrose or sugar, and potassium iodine to prevent goiter, a swelling in the neck.

While visits to both locations are fascinating (and highly recommended), I wanted to taste and see something closer to what Jesus and his disciples understood. Always craving salt *and* adventure, I found a place I could descend into an ancient seabed where salt seems frozen in time.

I drive 150 miles south to the Redmond Salt Mine and discover mountains of salt line the property like miniature Swiss Alps. Inside the main offices, I meet Neal, a late sixty-something with a youthful disposition despite his snowy hair. I'm curious how he became involved in the profession. He explains that after World War II, his father and uncle returned from the battlefield to work the family farm. But years of drought left them on the verge of bankruptcy.

One brother considered moving to Salt Lake City for work, the other to California. In their distress, they took one last walk across their property. Neal's father looked into the distance and took note of the salt mine on their neighbor's property. His eyes followed the landscape until they settled on their other neighbor's property, where another salt mine operated. He looked down, kicked the dirt, and had an idea.

They soon cleared a patch of cornfield and dug down. Thirty feet beneath the surface, they hit a salt vein that extended the entire length of their property and descended more than five thousand feet into the earth. On that day, Redmond Salt Mine was born. When you're caught between a rock and a hard place, God's provision is sometimes right beneath your toes.

When you're caught between a rock and a hard place, God's provision is sometimes right beneath your toes.

Neal started helping his dad and uncle by bagging salt at the age of eleven and has been in the family business ever since. He hands me a hard hat, and I snap the buckle beneath my chin as we climb into the company truck. Our first stop: the crushing mill, where salt first arrives from the mine.

Inside enormous bins, chunks of salt stack high according to their size. Larger boulders pass through a series of crushers until they're ground down to volleyball size. Then they're sorted for further milling.

The grinder refines salt according to its purpose. The bigger rocks will nourish wild game. The more refined ones are sold to ranchers to sustain livestock and restaurateurs to season entrées. Of the 2,500 tons of salt mined each day, the vast majority will de-ice roads across Utah and the Midwest during the winter months.

Inside the warehouse await pallets of products for purchase. Salt rocks for horses. Fortified mineral mix for goats. Salt nuggets for deer. Ice-melt for sidewalks. Bath salts for aching muscles. Table salt for cooking. Popcorn salt for snacking. I had no idea a single-sourced salt could be used for so many different purposes.

Toward the back of the property, we approach the entrance of the mine. Its square mouth yawns and swallows our truck whole. Natural daylight disappears, and a light sweetness wafts through the air. No wonder spending time in salt rooms is becoming so popular. As Neal drives us deeper into the salty earth, I close my eyes and breathe in the gentle scent.

When I reopen them, the sandstone cavern appears otherworldly. Crystals stretch down from the ceiling like frozen icicles. The salty stalactites form wherever water snakes through the ground above. Our descent is slow, as the road before us keeps forking. Every few minutes a large metal door opens to allow further passage.

"You'll want to pay attention," Neal advises. "If we get stranded down here, you'll need to remember the way out."

I stifle a panicky laugh. I have always been directionally challenged, and if we become stranded, I'm probably not the person who will find the exit sign. If survival depends on me, we may just have to see how well salt can preserve the human body in the bed of a pickup truck . . . underground . . . out of contact with all humanity.

The deeper we travel, the mustier the air becomes, like an old church basement. We're now 420 feet below the surface. We stop in front of a drilling machine, and the truck lights blink twice. The noisy drill stops and an eerie silence sets in. Bright white dust fills the air.

Climbing out of the vehicle, my feet crunch on the crystals as if I've landed on a beach. Neal leans over to click on my headlamp, and the ground glistens. This is a salt lover's paradise, and I pinch a sample. The crystals taste like nothing I've encountered before. The salt seems less abrasive and ends with a sweetish note.

Neal waves me toward the cavern wall. The fine particles still fall like snow. He brushes away a thin layer of salt dust to reveal the dazzling surface with colors of pink diamonds, peach garnets, and rose quartz. The natural cave art looks like it's been fashioned by the finest of jewelers.

And it has. To think God handcrafts such beauty in nooks and crannies throughout creation. The salt mine offers a rare glimpse. Such magnificence fills our planet, our solar system, our galaxy, and far, far beyond, and it all declares glory, glory, glory to God.

I want to stay longer, but I've interrupted the miners' operation, and they must return to work. On the drive toward the surface, I'm overwhelmed by the awe of being in a place that transcends my understanding of the world. Something about the depth and beauty of the salt mine reminds me that I am tiny and fragile. This happens whenever we become wonderstruck by creation: our emphasis on self automatically diminishes, and our desire to improve the welfare of others expands to occupy the space that ego once dwelled.

I squint as my eyes adjust to natural light.

"Are all salt mines that stunning?" I ask, breaking the silence.

As with snowflakes, Neal explains, no two salt mines are alike. Many appear bright white and produce colorless salt. The Redmond Mine's salt contains sixty trace minerals, and each act like a paintbrush. Swoops of rusty red come from the iron; the black speckles are evidence of manganese; magnesium adds a rosy hue. The combination of these and other elements creates the pinkish color and sweet flavor.

When we arrive at the headquarters, Neal's eyes narrow in concern. "I should have advised against wearing black."

I can't help but giggle. I look like Frosty the Snowman. A brush of the sleeve releases a poof of salt. The dust makes me cough but tastes so good.

After shaking off, I settle into a chair opposite Neal. We talk late into the afternoon. I'm reluctant to leave my new favorite place, but Neal makes it better by sending me home with chunks of salt rocks and instructions for transforming them into salt we can use in our kitchen.

I can't wait to test my salt-smashing skills.

THE JEWELED SYMBOLISM OF SALT IN SCRIPTURE

Much like the natural wonderment of the mine, salt glistens throughout the pages of the Bible. The first mention of salt in Scripture is also the most infamous. In Genesis, God rains down sulfur on Sodom, Gomorrah & Co. for debauchery and neglect of the poor. Lot's wife cranes her neck for a forbidden glimpse of the startling sight and transforms into a block of sodium chloride.

Like Utah, Israel and the surrounding region boast high concentrations of salt in areas such as the Dead Sea, the City of Salt, and the Valley of Salt—areas largely recognized as places where nothing sprouts, nothing grows. Jeremiah leans into this wasteland imagery when he says those who turn away from God will reside in a "salt land where no one lives."

The majority of salt's mentions appear far more positive. Salt symbolizes new beginnings and a separation from the past. Elisha tosses salt into a spring to purify the waters and signal a fresh start. The curse on the water is no more. Abimelech dumps salt on a captured city to represent a break from the past to forge a new way forward.

Ezekiel alludes to a rather strange practice using the fine grains. He describes rubbing newborns with salt as part of a baby's care after delivery. This is more than prophetic imagery: midwives of that time used salt as a natural loofa for removing any vernix, as well as to deter the growth of bacteria.

Salt is also added to the incense used in the tabernacle's daily worship. The divine recipe includes spices and minerals like stacte, onycha, galbanum, frankincense—and sodium too. The sacred perfume stimulates the Israelites' olfactory memories, signaling to their bodies, minds, spirits, and emotions the call to worship. God knew long before modern perfumers that salt unlocks a range of aromatic notes. Even today salt is added to scents to unearth fruity, floral, and citrus layers, as well as to accentuate the smokiness of woody aromas.

Moses tells the Israelites to add salt to their offerings, and in the process, the people agree to a "covenant of salt forever before the LORD." The Hebrew word for covenant, *běriyth*, means an agreement between two parties, based in trust, to fulfill their ends of the deal. The two parties of the covenant, God and his people, exchange salt, a tangible symbol of loyalty and friendship, to show the permanent nature of their agreement. Through salt, God reveals his indissoluble relationship with those he loves.

The Jewish people have not forgotten their salt covenants with God. To this day, every Friday at sunset, many practicing Jews still dip their bread into salt to keep their agreement with God.

Perhaps my love affair with salt is a reminder of something bigger.

JESUS SHAKES OUR UNDERSTANDING OF SALT

The moment I pull the screen from the kitchen window, Leif looks concerned.

"Just a little project, no worries," I assure him. He knows me well and appears unconvinced.

I gather the rest of my supplies: a hammer, safety glasses, clean cloth, parchment paper, disinfectant wipes, and a large salt rock. I use the parchment paper to create a clean surface. A self-professed germaphobe, I wipe down the hammer and screen three times with the wipes, then place the rock in the center of the paper, and *wham!*

The vibrations from impact cause salt granules and chunks to break free. *Wham! Wham!* The window screen doubles as a filter. I repeat the process of smashing then shaking the particles through the wire frame. Twenty-six minutes later, a cup and a half of freshly mined, freshly ground salt rests in my hand.

This collection is closer to what Jesus and his disciples enjoyed. None of the references to salt in Scripture refer to the highly refined, altered substance we're used to—fortified with iodine and chemicals since 1924. Biblical salt was always sourced and harvested with its surrounding minerals.

That becomes highly significant when Jesus declares, "You are the salt of the earth."

With these words, Jesus awakens each of us to our divine purpose. We are agents of preserving.

The curing practices that began in ancient Egypt quickly spread throughout Israel. Even the place where Jesus delivered this teaching as part of the Sermon on the Mount, overlooks the Sea of Galilee and Magdala, a town famed for the curing of fish. When Jesus mentions salt, everyone knew its primary role as a preservative.

In essence, Jesus tells his disciples and us today: We are agents of preserving. God has placed us in this culture, in this time, in this moment, in this slice of history, to preserve the ways, the teachings, the life, the power, the presence of Christ.

But salt does more than preserve; it also seasons, unlocking delicious flavor. While too much of a good thing can be a bad thing, the right amount of salt will create unforgettable dishes.

As the salt of the earth, we are agents of flavoring. Our purpose is to bring the taste of heaven to earth wherever we go. Salt improves flavors as it seasons. In low concentrations, salt suppresses bitterness and enhances sweetness; in higher concentrations, salt reduces sweetness but enhances umami and savory flavors. Just as salt brings out the best in food, so too, Christ brings out the best in us as others experience the flavor of Christ through us.

> Our purpose is to bring the taste of heaven to earth wherever we go.

Yes, as the salt of the earth, we are an important preserving agent and a vital flavoring agent, but we're also something more.

Jesus continues: "But if the salt loses its saltiness, how can it be made salty again? It is no longer good for anything, except to be thrown out and trampled underfoot."

Some commentators claim it's impossible for salt to lose saltiness. Once sodium chloride, always sodium chloride. Neal noted that none of those commentators ever worked in a salt mine.

Salt can, and does, lose its saltiness through the influx of other substances, he explained. When salt is overpowered, it loses its ability to perform as God designed, as an influencer.

Jesus's warning is designed to embolden us toward all aspects of our true purpose: We are the salt of the earth. We are an agent of preserving. We are an agent of flavoring. And the physician Luke adds yet another dimension of our salty purpose.

We discover this as he frames Jesus's teaching in slightly different terms. "Salt is good, but if it loses its saltiness, how can it be made salty again? It is fit neither for the soil nor for the manure pile; it is thrown out." This is a new twist, involving dirt and . . . *ahem* . . . smelly stuff.

Gardeners often wince at the idea of applying salt to soil, because large amounts will impoverish the land. But the proper amount of salt will cause plants to flourish. That's why both sodium and the salt substitute potassium chloride appear on the list of ingredients of Miracle Gro. It's not only humans who require salt to live; plants and soil need it too.

The Luke passage suggests that salt plays a role in manure, too. Salt helps break down fresh excrement for better plant absorption. The mineral also prevents dunghills from rotting and becoming useless for providing nutrients to crops.

Luke clarifies that when Jesus warns of losing our saltiness, he's not describing table salt; he's describing fertilizer salt. Yes, as the salt of the earth, we are agents of human flourishing. Jesus is calling us to be fertilizer in his kingdom. We are the salt poured on that which is foul in order to foster fresh, new life. We are created to help others blossom and bud as they pursue the life God intends. Flourishing lives demonstrate evidence of the kingdom of God.

"Salary" and "salad" aren't the only words derived from the Latin root *sal*, meaning salt. So too is the word "salvation."

Sometimes the places Christ sends you will feel manure-like—the last places, the last people, the last situations you'd ever want to engage. Like Jonah, you may be tempted to resist the hardship, the discomfort, the awkwardness and stinkiness, to stay in your comfort zone. Yet, it's your salty fertilizer that brings salvation to a dysfunctional and dying world.

And don't forget the kind of salt the disciples used was harvested with its surrounding minerals. Those trace elements gave the salt its uniqueness. In the same way, God uses you with all your naturally harvested "minerals"—your specific upbringing and personality and giftings and weaknesses and quirks. God leverages everything from your past wounds to your everyday work as he sprinkles you and other Jesus-followers throughout the world.

For me, it's hard to know where to begin some days. I become overwhelmed by the sheer quantity of needs that flood my inbox and mailbox, my texts and social media feeds. In search of how to find a way forward, I once stumbled on wisdom tucked into some ancient Jewish writings known as the Talmud. There it says that if someone is suffering and in need, and you can take away $\frac{1}{60}$ of their pain, then that is goodness, and the call to help is from God. This is a powerful expression of our being the salt—the preservers, the flavorers, the fertilizers—of the earth.

That fraction—$\frac{1}{60}$—is loaded with freedom. This liberates us from the pressured thinking that whispers, *Everything depends on you.* Your one little grain of salt can help with something someone else's grain can't. And when all the grains get mixed and sprinkled together, preserving and flavoring and helping others flourish occurs everywhere.

None of us are meant to preserve the whole earth, flavor the whole world, flourish the entire planet on our own. Yet you can begin today by simply asking God to bring to mind someone for whom you can ease $\frac{1}{60}$ of their pain. And don't be surprised if the person is closer than you think.

AROUND THE TABLE

Take a few moments in prayer to ask God to show you someone for whom you can ease ¹⁄₆₀ of their pain, beginning today. Most people are simply waiting for you to invite them into your life and give them the gift of your presence.

Write the name(s) God brought to mind on a piece of paper, along with how you'll ease their pain. Invite the person for coffee, a walk, a delightful activity. Send an encouraging note. Pick up the phone. Mail a care package.

LEIF'S SMOKED SALT

Smoked salt is a great addition to everyday cooking and also makes delightful gifts.

PREP: 10 minutes   **COOK:** 60 minutes   **COOL:** 10 minutes

2 cups wood chips, soaked in cold water for 1 hour, then drained
1 cup coarse salt

DIRECTIONS

1. Pour salt into aluminum foil pan and spread into a thin layer.
2. Choose your favorite wood chips—mesquite, apple, maple, or whatever you have on hand. On a charcoal grill, add the wood chips to the coals. On a gas grill, either place them in a smoker box or wrap them in a tightly sealed tinfoil packet.
3. Create indirect heat on the grill. If you're using a charcoal grill, place all the coals on one side and place the pan of salt on the cool side. If you're using a gas grill, heat the surface to medium and place the pan on a grate away from direct heat.
4. Cover the grill and smoke the salt at approximately 350 degrees for one hour.
5. Remove salt from heat and allow to cool. Pour into a jar and cover. Enjoy or give away.

Yields 1 cup smoked salt.

KARY'S DARK CHOCOLATE SEA SALT COOKIES (GLUTEN-FREE)

This is my favorite new cookie recipe because you don't need to apologize to anyone that these are gluten-free.

PREP: 10 minutes   **COOK:** 15–20 minutes   **COOL:** 10 minutes

3 cups powdered sugar
3/4 cup unsweetened dark chocolate cocoa powder
1/4 teaspoon fine salt
1/2 teaspoon salt flakes
4 large egg whites at room temperature
2 teaspoons vanilla
parchment paper
Optional: 2 1/2 cups walnuts and 1 cup peanut butter chips

DIRECTIONS

1. Preheat oven to 350. Line two baking sheets with parchment paper.
2. In a large bowl, mix powdered sugar, cocoa powder, and fine salt. Add egg whites and vanilla and whisk together until most clumps disappear. If you over-whisk, the batter will stiffen. Spoon onto baking sheet in 20–24 different cookies. Sprinkle a few salt flakes on each cookie.
3. Bake cookies 15–18 minutes. Pull from oven when cookies become glossy, firm to the touch, and cracked on the surface.

4. Slide the parchment paper on two wire cooling racks. Use a spatula to loosen the cookies from the parchment paper shortly after they come out of the oven.

Makes 20–24 cookies.

Bonus: Leif prefers to add 2$\frac{1}{2}$ cups of walnut halves and 1 cup of peanut butter chips to the recipe. We'll often bake our cookies side by side and when we share them, we'll ask people to vote between Team Margaret and Team Leif to decide which is best. We'd love to know your vote! If you try both recipes, email us at hello@margaretfeinberg.com and let us know which you prefer.

CAROLYN'S OOEY-GOOEY SALTED CHOCOLATE CHIP COOKIES

These soft, chocolatey cookies will quickly become a favorite.

PREP: 20 minutes, **COOK:** 20 minutes **COOL:** 10 minutes plus 24–36 hours
of refrigeration

2 cups minus 2 tablespoons cake flour
1$\frac{2}{3}$ cups bread flour
1$\frac{1}{4}$ teaspoons baking soda
1$\frac{1}{2}$ teaspoons baking powder
1$\frac{1}{2}$ teaspoons coarse salt
1$\frac{1}{4}$ cups unsalted butter
1$\frac{1}{4}$ cups light brown sugar, packed
1 cup plus two tablespoons granulated sugar
2 large eggs
2 teaspoons real vanilla extract
1$\frac{1}{4}$ pounds chocolate chips (semi-sweet, dark, or whatever
    you prefer)
pinch of sea salt
Optional: pecans, dried cherries, ice cream

DIRECTIONS

1. Mix flours, baking soda, baking powder, and coarse salt into a bowl. Set aside.

2. In a mixer, cream butter and sugars together (about 5 minutes). Add eggs—mixing well after each addition. Stir in vanilla.
3. On low, add dry ingredients (5–10 seconds).
4. Drop in chocolate chips (and/or pecans and cherries).
5. Cover with plastic wrap and refrigerate for 24–36 hours.
6. Preheat oven to 350 degrees. Line a baking sheet with parchment paper.
7. Scoop 36 half golf-ball sized cookies onto the baking sheet. Sprinkle with sea salt.
8. Bake until golden brown but still soft (about 18–20 minutes).
9. Cool on wire rack for 10 minutes. Serve warm or with vanilla ice cream.

Makes 36 cookies.

A Bowl of Delectable Olives

TASTE AND SEE GOD'S HEALING

My body rotates around a tree until I pluck every last olive. Two hours and fifty-seven minutes have passed since I first tried my hand at this. I relish in how my skills are improving, but then I look to my seventy-five-year-old companion, Mama. She has cleared two and a half trees in the same span of time.

Leif and I have never visited Croatia before, but when Natalija (pronounced Nah-tall-yah), who is Mama's daughter, extends an invitation to harvest olives, we travel to the island of Hvar. Underneath swooping brown bangs, Natalija's round sapphire eyes sparkle with life. When I glimpse gray cartoon socks peeking beneath her pant hem, I know we'll become fast friends.

We cram our overstuffed suitcases into a jellybean-sized car and drive into the village. Her bleach-white home perches on the side of a hill blossoming with fruit. A kiwi tree shades the lower entrance and grape vines snake along the stairs. Leaves of an orange tree brush our shoulders as we approach the front door. Leif notices me salivating and mutters that I shouldn't get any bright ideas. We depart in a few days, and "fruit thief" doesn't look great to customs agents.

Natalija gives us a tour of the house. On the bottom floor, she catches me eyeing a collection of empty plastic soda bottles and glass jam jars. Unlike commercial sellers who bottle and seal their products, her family sometimes gives their oil to friends to make homemade products. They store their liquid in large stone containers, and these plastic and glass vessels transport the smaller quantities.

The stockpile reminds me of the widow who pleads with Elisha. Unable to pay her debts, the creditors come to handcuff her sons and traffic them as slaves. The prophet asks what payment she can offer. Everything is gone, she reveals, except for one vial of olive oil. Elisha instructs the widow to request containers from anyone and everyone. The community rallies. Neighbors rummage for all the mugs and jugs they can find. The mismatched collection piles high.

The widow closes her front door. In the dimness, the sons watch as their mother empties the vial of oil into an oversized container. A gasp sweeps through the home as the oil flows in abundance. The widow reaches for a second vessel, and that one fills too. Jaws drop as the oil, which brings much gladness, gushes before their eyes. When all the containers fill to the brim, the supply runs dry. The miraculous abundance buys the sons' freedom from slavery, breaks the cycle of poverty, heals the family, and leaves the community flabbergasted.

Natalija's collection expands my appreciation for the jar-hoarding widow. Thousands of years later, people still gather jars from their communities to transport and sell oil.

We rise before the sun the next morning, expectant of all we will taste and see. Natalija explains that her family can't afford to miss a day of harvesting. She and her mom harvest the trees; her dad stays home to clear leaves and stems. They must pick all their olives before the mill shuts down for the season.

After a breakfast of bread dipped in olive oil, we begin the hour drive toward the trees. The tangerine hues of the sunrise linger as the village disappears in the rearview window. Our tiny car sputters along hairpin turns as we ascend the island's higher hills. The road turns to gravel and narrows. In a moment of weakness, I peer down the cliff inches from our car's tires. I shut my eyes and focus on counting my breaths. Heights have never been my friend.

Leif nudges me that it's safe to look. When I do, gnarled trees boasting gray silvery leaves flicker in the wind. Some appear so heavy with olives, their branches almost touch the ground. Others stretch lightly fruited stems skyward. Within each trunk are whorls of wood grain, which like clouds, resemble faces or familiar forms.

Natalija slows whenever we pass an elderly couple picking along the roadside. She shouts something friendly out the window, then skids by. In this agrarian community, everyone knows everyone. The car eases to a halt and Natalija announces our arrival. Unlike modern orchards, these trees were never planted in tidy rows. The crooked lines of trees expand outward in all directions like a tangled fishing net.

"This is one of our fields," Natalija beams.

"Where do we start?" I ask, feeling overwhelmed.

She points to specific trees up the hillside: "That one, those two, and a few that way."

"I thought you owned them all." I fail to hide my relief.

"We're not rich," Natalija laughs. "The trees belong to different families. My great grandfather bought these long ago."

We unload five-gallon buckets filled with folded tarps and hike the steep mountainside. The trees have been traded and bartered for centuries. Families have passed them down to their children and grandchildren, but with each generation the size of the parcel decreases. If a family owns a dozen trees, then the six children receive two each. The result is a complex patchwork quilt of properties, some consisting of only a single tree.

Centuries of harsh weather, wild vegetation, and neglect chew through the crumbling rock walls between the olive trees. The result is a land fractured into a maze of rocky separations. Studying the miles of labyrinth, I recall an ancient Proverb: "Don't cheat your neighbor by moving the ancient boundary markers set up by previous generations."

Natalija explains no one in this community would dare pick another person's tree or claim another tree as their own. Such actions would wound relationships and fracture the community. The unmoved stones serve as living reminders of the importance of respecting, remembering, and honoring the past as well as ensuring the future.

As we approach the first tree, an aged, squatty woman descends a ladder. She wears an unbuttoned, tattered cardigan, and flashes a toothless smile. This is Natalija's mother, who speaks only Croatian.

"Mama!" I shout as if I'm in a Greek wedding movie. She embraces us with breasty hugs.

Hunger and curiosity drive me to pluck an olive for tasting. I spew the bitter fragments from my tongue. Mama laughs. I learn the twisty-faced way not to eat olives fresh from a tree. They must be cured with salt, lye, or brine to become tasty.

Natalija explains that olives transition through a spectrum of colors as they ripen. The bright green ones resemble mini sour apples. The reddish ones look like cherries. The blackish ones, many of which dot the ground, contain the most oil.

I start picking, then hesitate. "Which olives should I pick first?"

"All of them," Natalija assures.

About this time, Mama approaches me and mutters something incomprehensible.

She slides her hand up the branch as if she's romancing the tree. With a swift gliding motion, her fingers descend. More than a dozen olives plop into her bucket. The approach protects the fruit and branch tips, both crucial for producing high-quality oil. Bruised olives yield higher acidity and less desirable oil; broken tips reduce new growth for next year. I emulate her gentle ways, but alas, the thin branch cracks and leaves fly in all directions. Three lonely olives plonk into my pail. Mama tosses me an encouraging wink.

I reach for a fallen leaf, rub its velvety texture, inhale its earthy scent. The leaf frames a mini-miracle, a microcosm of divine marvel. Olive leaves contain tiny hairs around their pores that shape themselves to accommodate changing seasons. These shape-shifting hairs enable the leaves to open flat in the moist season and curl inward during dry spells. This explains why the same olive tree boasts sea-green leaves one month and slate-gray the next.

Besides the rustle of branches, we labor mostly in silence. Donkeys whine faintly in the distance. A solo car hums past. The long hours provide time to reflect on the olive's place in history. Many believe olive trees rank among the first domesticated plants. More than eight hundred million olive trees dot the surface of planet Earth today, and almost 90 percent are located in the Mediterranean region. Several countries in the Middle East still squabble over who owns the oldest living olive tree, but then again, squabbling is considered something of a sport there.

Olives enjoy a rich, lush history. The Egyptians used olive oil along with salt in their mummifying process. The Greeks created the original Olympic flame from burning olive branches, and the heads of champions were adorned with olive wreath crowns.

For Christians in a post-Roman world, olive oil provided a holy symbol. The faithful found their identity, their mark of belonging, in the olive. Monasteries used olives for sacraments, food, and lighting, which provided a way to honor martyrs who had been burned alive in oil for their faith.

The influence of the olive extends into philosophy, science, literature, and art. Aristotle told stories about olives, and Leonardo invented a more efficient olive press. Homer, Dante, even Shakespeare wrote about olives. Van Gogh painted eighteen images of olives while Renoir almost refused to paint them, noting that when light hits an olive tree it sparkles like diamonds, and the changing hues are "enough to drive you mad."

The olive tree was one of the first Old World plants to be rooted in America. The agricultural skills of the Dominican, Jesuit, and Franciscan missionaries brought olives into South America, then Mexico, then Alta, California, in the late eighteenth century. Friars planted olive trees in San Diego in 1760 for oil to lubricate machinery, prepare wool to spin, make soap, cook, light, and of course, anoint. Olives gained widespread popularity in America after the emergence of the Mediterranean Diet in the 1950s. Today, television chefs have made olives and "EVOO" (Extra Virgin Olive Oil) a mainstay in countless kitchens.

Here on the island of Hvar, olives are a way of life. We work until mid-afternoon, when Natalija transforms the olive tarp into a picnic blanket under the tree's shade. Mama unpacks a pouch of mandarin oranges, a cut of meat, a loaf of crusty bread, and a cylinder of black and green Oblica olives steeped in oil.

Natalija explains that while wine improves with age, oil does not. When first pressed, olive oil tastes sharp and peppery but mellows after two to three months. Store for more than a year and rancidity sets in. Some olive oils can last a few years, but they must be filtered for purity and stored in dark glass bottles that protect from light and heat. That's why Natalija uses the blackish bottle with a tight seal for her personal stock.

Table Discovery: Extra virgin olive oil is perfect for low-temperature cooking up to 320 degrees, and regular olive oil for medium heat up to 420 degrees. If you ever feel overwhelmed by which olive oil to choose, guidance awaits at 1–800-OLIVE-OIL.

Much like sommeliers, Natalija explains, olive connoisseurs compare, contrast, and argue over their favorite types. Some prefer dark Greek Kalamatas for their snappiness; others, the Italian Castelvetranos, with their Kermit-green color and buttery flesh; still others, the French Nicoise for their assertiveness. The olive varietals are also enjoyed as oils. Some prefer the peppery taste of Tuscan oil or the fruity Luccas or the sharp bitters of the Chianti region.

Natalija says everyone on her island believes their oil is the best, and their bias is difficult to deny. Plopping an oily olive into my mouth, I attempt to describe the flavors that splash across my tongue in quick waves. "Sharp, almost astringent, with a nutty aftertaste." Leif uses words like "bitter," "chewy," and "almondy." Natalija translates our descriptions to Mama who says, "*Dobro, dobro*," meaning "Good, good." We nod in hearty agreement and munch on more.

I later learn that the International Olive Oil Council has compiled a list of terms to describe the nuances of oil for foodies. Descriptions include *aggressive*, *assertive*, or *pungent*; *bitter*, *delicate*, or *gentle*; *rustic*, *spicy*, or *sweet*.

Perhaps it's the hard work or perhaps it's the pleasure of eating outdoors, but the simple meal satisfies. Food somehow always tastes better under these conditions. Fish always tastes better when you catch it, fruit when you pluck it, bread when you knead it, and salt when you grind it. The invested time and hard work make everything more delicious.

Invested time and hard work make everything more delicious.

We soon return to work: Massage the olives from the branch. Collect the fruit in buckets. Empty the tarp's contents. Carry to the car. Repeat.

Mama uses an ax to trim the branches after we complete clearing a tree. Sometimes she takes short breaks to talk to Leif. And by talk, I mean she gestures with exaggerated motions and shouts with increasing volume. She seems convinced that if she speaks loud enough, Leif will magically understand Croatian. With mounting frustration, she stops abruptly and wraps her wrinkled body around Leif in a hug.

She's been trying to express her gratitude. At a height of 6'8" and with extra-long arms, Leif can harvest branches Mama could never reach without climbing a ladder.

I become more comfortable picking with each passing hour. I climb to precarious limbs to reach the tallest branches. A hearty brush of cold wind knocks me off balance. I wrap my body around the trunk, then swing from a branch with glee. Mama guffaws, proof that silliness translates to any language.

HOW OLIVES BUD IN THE BIBLE

Of all the elements I've tasted and seen in Scripture, none has proven more healing and sensual than olives and their oil. This fruit of a tree bursts with a sharp, savory zest, then transforms into a buttery coolness, much like its presence in the Bible.

The olive makes its scriptural debut when Noah, whose name means "comfort," awakes miserable and nauseated. It's not hard to imagine his feeling this way while imprisoned aboard a vessel full of agitated animals and their unending piles of manure. All those beasts and scaled creatures moan and groan, squeak and reek. Noah and his family work around the clock to scrape the detritus overboard, but the rocking and rolling, combined with the stink, make Noah want to hurl. Everything becomes far worse than Noah ever imagined, ever predicted. *Why was I named Comfort? What a lousy namesake!*

In desperation to rest his sea-weary legs, Noah sends out birds who almost forgot how to fly. A lone dove returns clenching an olive branch in its beak. Both the branch and dove become symbols of peace and spark hope in Noah's tired bones. In that beautiful moment, God hand-delivers *pax* on *pax*, *shalom* on *shalom*, peace on peace, giving us hope that in the painful storms of life, God will heal us with his deep peace, too.

Olives continue to make surprising appearances throughout the Bible. After his people escape Egyptian slavery, God folds the flavor of olive oil into the manna. This provides the Israelites a taste of comfort, of the familiar, as they spiral through the desert. The flavor assuages the pain of where they've been and alerts their taste buds to the healing ahead. The land they're promised will abound in wheat and barley, vines and figs, pomegranates and olive groves.

While massaging the drupes from the branches, I'm reminded of the myriad ways God reveals his healing presence to the Israelites through olives. Israel is named "a green olive tree, beautiful in fruit and form;" and the righteous are compared to strong olive trees. Even their children are likened to shoots from the trees' roots. To this day, the Hebrew idiom for a good man is "pure olive oil."

Table Discovery: New to olives? Many varieties exist far beyond the canned version you see atop pizza or on the nacho platter. Head to your local grocer. Often newer groceries like Whole Foods and Sprouts will include olive bars. Pick up some large Cerignola olives which are mild, not too salty, and delicious plain. Next try some purplish Kalamata olives, which are saltier than green olives and provide a bold taste. You'll be well on your way to becoming an olive connoisseur.

With each cleared branch, my fingers dew with oil. I remember that in Scripture olive oil illuminates the tabernacle and Solomon's temple. The ever-lit oil in the temple reminds the Israelites of Moses's encounter with the burning bush and their hard-won journey from slavery to freedom. Oil drips from the chins of priests and kings, those set apart to serve and bring healing to the land. Israel's first king, Saul, glows with oil during his coronation. David, too, anointed by Samuel, glimmers with liquid gold. The shepherd-king makes the store and care of olives a national concern. Baal-Hanan manages olive trees; Joash, the storage and supply of oil.

The priests catch whiffs of olive scent as oil drips into the grain and wave offerings. The cherubim, who overshadow the ark of the covenant in the holy of holies, have been carved from olivewood and overlaid with gold. And in the temple, the carpenters have fashioned four-faced, winged cherubs made from olivewood into the doors.

Isaiah prophesies the greatest display of God's healing will come from a shoot on Jesse's stump. The prophet's descriptions of the shoots resemble the way an olive tree grows. This is no ordinary olive sprig, because the Spirit of God will rest on this one in abundance.

The name of that shoot?

Jesus.

Just before sunset, a passing storm whips the wind and spews its first droplets.

"*Yaa, yaa!*" Mama shouts, urging us toward the vehicles.

We scurry like mice, grabbing the last fistfuls of olives, then our tools and wood trimmings. I attempt to carry one of the buckets of olives to the car, but my arms feel too tired, my shoulders too sore. Leif scoops up the weight with ease. I grab a few pieces of wood instead. Unlike the firewood from pine trees on the island, which burns fast, olivewood burns slow.

"We waste nothing," Natalija says. "Never the wood. This will keep us warm this winter."

Once back at Natalija's, my head hits the pillow with a skull thud. I collapse into bed exhausted and achy, well aware that I've been whupped by a seventy-five-year-old woman named Mama.

THE HEALING YOUR HEART CRAVES

The next evening, we gather around a wobbly table spread with a familiar menu of the island's staples—pomegranates, oranges, bread, meat, and of course, a bowl of delectable olives sopping in oil. I often read of the repetitive nature of the ancient diet, and now I am experiencing it firsthand.

As we chat, the lamplight catches Natalija's glimmering skin. She radiates with the beauty of a woman twenty years younger.

"What's your secret?" I prod.

Natalija shares that she never uses any creams for her skin, only olive oil, because of its anti-aging properties. The oil absorbs easily, and if she desires a fresh scent, she adds rose or lavender. She tells of a woman on a nearby island who has become so obsessed with Natalija's olive oil that she orders multiple liters every fall. She spends thirty minutes each day lathered in the oil before showering to allow her skin to heal and shine.

Natalija doesn't realize she's describing the beauty practices of ancient queens of the Bible. After Queen Vashti snubs her husband, King Xerxes searches for a remarkable replacement. Esther, a young Jewish woman, travels along with other beautiful young women to the kingdom to receive twelve months of beauty treatments. The first half of the year includes treatments of oil with myrrh, followed by six months of perfumes and cosmetics, many of which have olive oil as their base.

Esther shines with a beauty that catches the king's eye, and later, as queen, she goes on to save her people. Millennia later, Natalija serves as a living embodiment of Esther's beauty regimen.

Maybe Esther and Natalija are onto something God has known all along. At the table, I recognize *this* is the sacramental nature of olives: through them, we are reminded of God's *healing* power.

Though I feel tired and sore from long work days, I rub my hands together and discover that where I should feel the damage of blisters and callouses beginning to form, I instead find smooth, soft, and supple skin. It's as if I've been at a world-class spa with someone soaking my palms in the world's finest oil all day. I've always known olive oil serves as a physical *symbol* of healing, but now I'm learning that it has literal healing capabilities, too. The oil of olives heals dry skin here in Croatia, in the arid Middle East of the Bible, and—I hope—in the desert of Utah too, where my skin tends to shrivel and crack.

I discover that the healing properties of olives reach more than skin deep. Olives heal us from the inside out. The oil contains oleocanthal, an anti-inflammatory which acts like the common pain reliever ibuprofen. The oil can slow the aging in bones and the pain in joints. Even the leaves of the olive trees hold healing properties. Recent studies have shown olive leaves possess anti-viral, anti-bacterial, and antioxidant properties.

When asked how she became the oldest living person in the world at 119, Jeanne Calment cited olive oil as her secret. She rubbed spoonfuls into her skin daily and consumed it at nearly every meal. "I have only one wrinkle, and I am sitting on it," she quipped.

At one of her birthday parties, a journalist said, "Well, I guess I will see you next year," to which Jeanne responded, "I don't see why not; you look to be in pretty good health."

When in Israel, I never spotted olive oil in the pharmacy aisles, but one day my fishing buddy Ido started to develop a cold. When I asked if I could help him with anything, he sent me to the kitchen to retrieve a glass of olive oil. Ido drank half right away, smacked his lips, and announced with bravado, "I do this every time I start to get sick. The olive heals, you know."

THE CRUSHING OF AN OLIVE MILL

The rest of the week follows the same routine of olive picking on other mountain slopes, until our final day, when Leif and I crowd into Natalija's car along with Papa to carry thousands of olives across the island for processing.

We arrive at the red brick mill, and when climbing out of the car, I struggle to find my footing. The roads around the mill are covered with slippery oil. "No smoking" signs appear everywhere. I assume it's because the oil is a fire hazard, but Natalija explains that olive oil takes on the surrounding scents. If a person smokes near the mill, then the whole batch will taste like cigarettes.

The owner recognizes Papa and waves us inside. Eight men scramble to empty the vehicle, pour olives into crates, and weigh the contents to determine their share of the oil. The hopper fills with olives, where they are further cleaned of debris. Grinders crush the pulp and pits into a mash that looks like a yummy tapenade, but I know better than to sneak a taste. The mash moves through a centrifuge, where hot water separates oil from the olives' natural water content. Soon the precious liquid pours through a narrow spout.

The modern press offers many advancements, but the principles for extracting olive oil remain the same as in antiquity: crush, knead, extract. Then and now, the olives must pass through a press where they writhe and wrestle under pressure to produce the oil that feeds, illuminates, and heals.

The process at the olive mill reminds me of Jesus's visit to an olive press. On the evening of his betrayal, Jesus retreats to pray at the Mount of Olives in the Garden of Gethsemane, a place that means olive press or olive yard. He could have gone anywhere, such as holing up with friends like Mary, Martha, and Lazarus and enjoying the comforts of their nearby home in Bethany. Instead, the "Anointed One" spends his last night on earth among olive trees, wrestling with the Father about his mission and destiny.

Jesus knows the raw brutality of the hours ahead and begs for another way, *any* other way. The acute anxiety crushes his body from the inside out as Jesus experiences hematidrosis, or blood sweat. The bright red secretions likely appeared on his forehead, beneath his nails, in his tears. His skin would have become vulnerable and fragile. Mark mentions that Jesus falls to the ground; he may have bled from the point of impact.

"Father, if you are willing, take this cup from me," Jesus petitions.

To this request, there is no response. Jesus yields to the silence and surrenders to the Father's intention: "Yet not my will, but yours be done."

From here he walks the long, silent road of obedience toward death. Before Jesus bleeds from the cross, he bleeds in the olive garden. As an olive must writhe and wrestle under intense pressure to yield oil, so too the Savior of the world writhes and wrestles until from him flows an inexhaustible supply of grace, anointing, and healing.

Months before Jesus walked this tumultuous path, he told a story about a man who found himself imperiled along the road to Jericho. In the parable of the good Samaritan, Jesus describes a man brutalized and left for dead in a roadside ditch. Lofty leaders pass by, each carrying a mental checklist of why it's better not to become involved. Then an untamed, unnamed man enters the scene with God's healing in his wings. He disinfects the wounds with wine and pours the healing salve of olive oil over each gash before taking the man to long-term care. Finishing the story, Jesus, the "Anointed One," instructs us to go and do likewise.

Then Jesus sends out disciples two by two with instructions to travel light. They anoint sick people with oil, and many whom they slather are healed. The Anointed One calls us to anoint and be anointed with oil in all our ailments, as well. Even though olive oil isn't a magic potion, anointing people is a practice rooted deep in Scripture as an act of compassion, an expression of love, an invitation to healing. If anyone among us is sick, we should call on the church's overseers to anoint us with oil and pray.

Years ago, I traveled to Honduras as part of a conference prayer team. I stood near the front with my prayer partner, Elizabeth, as people streamed forward. A woman approached us and described a growth in her throat that caused excessive pain. Elizabeth painted a cross with olive oil on the woman's forehead, and we prayed for God's healing. After a few minutes, the woman asked to sit down on a pew and then lay down on the ground in response to Jesus's healing presence. When I placed my hand lightly on her throat, I felt the bulbous mass protruding from beneath her skin. Elizabeth and I continued to petition the Anointed One to heal her. We knew the oil wasn't a magical potion and that neither of us had the power to heal on our own. All we knew was that Jesus had instructed his disciples to anoint and pray.

Our words felt intense, as if we were knocking on the doors of heaven and beating back the gates of hell. When the woman opened her eyes, she reached toward her neck and said, "The pain is gone—I've been healed."

Only I didn't believe her.

"Are you sure?" I kept asking.

"*Si, si, si,*" she said. "*Curado!*"

Elizabeth and I needed proof, so we tapped her neck as if we were physicians. The mass had vanished and her pain along with it. We crouched over the woman in disbelief.

Later, I confessed to Elizabeth that I didn't think God would heal the woman. Elizabeth felt the same way. We had asked God to heal out of obedience, not faith, and Jesus healed her anyway.

Healing remains a mystery. Sometimes we obey Jesus by anointing and praying, and people return to full health; other times the sickness and suffering remain. The healing of the Anointed One doesn't flow in the way or timeframe for which we often grievously ache. I know this firsthand as someone who lives in chronic pain.

I have asked God to heal me for years, and I sometimes become despondent in the affliction. Some days the pain is better, sometimes worse. Despite the pain, Jesus sends us out like the disciples to anoint and pray regardless of the immediate, visible outcome.

We are called to be people who give and receive anointing and prayer. The act itself can be healing as we make ourselves vulnerable, allow someone to enter our space and physically touch us, to remind us that we are not alone.

Any healing we see or experience is a gift from God, a glimpse of the future we've been promised.

In the fullness of time, God promises we will experience the fullness of healing. Sometimes the wait feels unbearable. Olives and their oil remind us to stay hungry to what's possible and coming with God. Like the widow, we are to set out our jars alongside each other that God might fill us in ways we never thought possible.

Before we leave the island of Hvar, Natalija informs of us of a common practice within the olive community: Those who harvest receive one liter of oil for each day worked. Knowing how much this will cost her family, I resist. Yet Natalija insists and hands us a stack of soda bottles full of olive oil, with instructions to transfer the liquid into a dark glass container as soon as we arrive home.

With a full heart, I receive the bottles of oil and tuck them into my bag. On the ferry back to the mainland, Leif leans against the window for a much-needed catnap, but I'm still buzzing with energy. I check social media on my phone until my cell service dies, then I play a game on my computer until my battery dies. I review my notes from the trip, journal a few pages, and pace the deck. But then curiosity sparks and I retrieve one of Natalija's bottles.

I loosen the cap of the holy gift, arch my neck downward, and breathe in its buttery scent. These bottles contain more than oil; they are full of memories. My olfactory receptors fire, triggering remembrances from our Croatian whirlwind trip. I think of Mama and I think of Natalija. I recall the hard days and the soft skin on my hands. I remember the grove and the harvest and the mill. I am reminded of Elizabeth and the healing of the woman in Honduras. I consider the healing that has taken place in my body, in my heart, in my relationships, and the healing I still long for. I think of Jesus, the Anointed One, who writhed and wrestled for our sake. For our healing.

AROUND THE TABLE

Place a bottle of olive oil on the table and invite everyone to join in the following prayer:

> *Blessed are you, Lord, our God, King of the universe, who creates the fruit of the tree. Heal me, O Lord, and I shall be healed; save me, and I shall be saved, for you are my praise. Amen.*

Hand out photocopies of the download at

www.margaretfeinberg.com/tasteandsee,

along with pens. Invite everyone to spend a few moments asking God to reveal any areas that need healing. Write down names, places, memories, or regrettables that come to mind. Ask God to heal each one.

Then invite each person to share aloud one area of personal pain. When the first person has finished, someone else should use a dab of olive oil to anoint the sharer's forehead or arm as a symbol of Christ's presence in suffering as the Anointed One. Pray a blessing over the one who has been anointed with oil. Repeat until everyone at the table has received prayer.

JESSICA'S OLIVE OIL DIJON DRESSING

This tangy dressing is a must-have on salads, veggies, or in your favorite wrap.

PREP: 3 minutes   **COOK:** none   **COOL:** none

2 tablespoons whole grain Dijon mustard
2 tablespoons freshly squeezed lemon juice
2 tablespoons apple cider vinegar
4 tablespoons extra virgin olive oil
pinch of pepper and garlic powder, to taste

DIRECTIONS

1. Mix ingredients thoroughly and pour over your favorite salad or roasted veggies.
2. Save extra dressing in a sealed container in the fridge.

Makes 1/2 cup dressing.

MARGARET'S BASIL OLIVE OIL DIP

This fast and simple olive oil dip goes well with freshly baked bread.

PREP: 5 minutes   **COOK:** 3 minutes   **COOL:** none

1/2 cup olive oil
1/2 cup fresh basil leaves
1 tablespoon garlic salt
1 tablespoon Parmesan cheese
1/2 teaspoon salt
1/2 teaspoon pepper
Optional: 1/4 teaspoon red pepper flakes
1 loaf fresh bread

DIRECTIONS

1. Chop basil finely. Gently mix basil, garlic salt, parmesan cheese, salt, pepper, and red pepper flakes. Add olive oil.
2. Serve olive oil dip and fresh bread as an appetizer or as part of the meal.

Makes 3/4 cup of olive oil dip.

CHRISTY'S FIG-OLIVE TAPENADE

This is the perfect sweet and savory combination to add to a cheese board or a center snack at your dinner gathering. Leif and I love the savory sweetness of this spread.

PREP: 15 minutes **COOK:** none   **COOL:** none

1/2 cup pitted Kalamata olives
1/2 cup stemmed and halved dried figs (about 8 figs)
2 teaspoons capers
1 teaspoon chopped garlic
2 teaspoons fresh thyme leaves, plus more for garnish
2 tablespoons olive oil
2 teaspoons balsamic vinegar
kosher salt and freshly ground black pepper, to taste
bread or crackers

DIRECTIONS

1. Pulse olives, figs, capers, garlic, and thyme in a food processor until a coarse mixture forms. Add olive oil, balsamic, salt, and pepper, and pulse to combine.
2. Serve with your favorite cracker or a fresh piece of French baguette.

Makes 1 cup of dip.

A Flame-Grilled Lamb Chop

TASTE AND SEE GOD'S RESCUE

I may be an *aspiring* foodie, but I'm an *actual* carnivore. Seriously. If I were a dinosaur, I'd be a T-Rex. Apologies to all my vegan readers.

I salivate at the scent of a sizzling steak. Perhaps that's why Leif and I have multiple grills on our back porch—a wood pellet, a smoker, and gas for speedy meals. To me, few foods warrant a celebration like a salty slab of beef ripped off a sizzling grill. The flavorful crust, slight chew, the tenderness, the juiciness, and the aroma create an unforgettable multisensory experience. Most people opt for a filet mignon or rib eye; I'm on a perpetual hunt for a well-marbled New York strip.

Given my obsession with steak, you can imagine how excited I was to hear rumors of a fanatical butcher outside Dallas who calls himself the "Meat Apostle." His name is Matt Hamilton and he owns a modest butcher shop in downtown McKinney called Local Yocal. Don't be tricked by the store's unassuming appearance. On the front patio, Matt runs something of a carnivore college where he teaches his gospel of sustainable meat eating to hungry disciples from across the globe.

The legend of the Meat Apostle sounds too eccentric to be true, so I enroll in his "Steakology 101" class and board a plane for Dallas to see for myself.

From the moment I arrive, Matt lives up to all the hype and more. With his straw cowboy hat and all-American smile, he entertains guests like a Wild West carnival showman. He plays up his love for college football and God and everything red, white, and blue. If Matt's personality is any indication, everything is indeed bigger in Texas.

It's all fun and games as the new students roll in, but the tone grows more serious when the class commences. Instead of a big chalkboard, we face a lineup of oversized black outdoor grills. Picnic tables double as desks as we are encouraged to take notes. The information comes at us hard and fast. The whole event feels less like a lecture and more like a revival.

For three and a half hours, the Meat Apostle preaches about the plight of today's rancher, sermonizes about the importance of ethical treatment of animals, and teaches us how to identify cuts of meat. His charismatic presentation leaves us hanging on each word. Even when the mesquite smokes into charcoal embers, no one complains about the air-to-wear humidity of the July afternoon.

My stomach turns queasy when Matt segues into the high cost of cheap meat. With razor-thin margins, the life span of a steer has been reduced from four to five years in the 1930s to just over one year today. Growing a calf from eighty pounds to twelve hundred pounds in fourteen months requires shortcuts: excessive amounts of corn and grain, growth hormones, and multiple rounds of anti-biotics because the animals become prone to more illness.

"Guess what they do with the weakest and unhealthiest cows?"

No one raises a hand.

"Hamburger . . ." he says, ". . . but do you know what's in those patties?"

My stomach performs an involuntary backflip.

"More than you want to know."

The average pound of hamburger from the grocery store includes the DNA of 60–130 different cows. That's how one sick animal can spur massive meat recalls and affect thousands of meals. Lifting up a pound of Local Yocal's burger meat, Matt announces, "This is one cow and no other cow."

Matt touts the genetic history of the cow tracing back more than fifty years. He knows the lineage, how the cow's ancestors were treated and bred, their birth date, wean date, and processing date. The meat at Matt's store is raised and butchered using the most humane techniques. And if an animal ever needs antibiotics, they wait at least a year to process her so none of those drugs affect consumers.

Toward the final hour of class, an aroma rises from the grill. Few scents make me as hungry as the smell of roasting meat. The sweet-salty beefiness fills our nostrils and the class circles the grills in anticipation. We taste sausage and lamb and obscure cuts of steak. The class ends without an invitation, altar call, or corporate prayer, but by the time we are dismissed, I have repented of my unhealthy habits and converted to a new way of consuming meat. I can't wait to share my discoveries with all my foodie friends.

WHERE ANCIENT FOOD REGULATIONS
SHOW UP TODAY

I ask Matt if he's willing to answer some questions about meat in
Scripture. Rather than convene at his butcher shop, we meet in a
gutted warehouse down the street. He plans to transform the space
into a new location for community building and education, a connecting point for people who want to prepare and consume food
more thoughtfully.

Matt talks fast with sweeping gestures, but he's not the same carny
entertainer I witnessed before. This is a gastro-visionary. Matt
points toward an area designed for larger classes. I follow him
through two kitchens—one for wood-fired pizzas and another for
grilling steaks.

"We're creating the mecca of meat!" he announces.

Leaning back in an office chair, he removes his signature cowboy hat
dotted with an American flag pin, revealing strawberry blonde hair.

I'm curious what Matt thinks of ancient food regulations.
Throughout the Torah, God instructs how to eat, when to eat, what
to eat, and how much to eat. Some foods are prohibited; others
permissible. Insects qualify as kosher, so long as they jump, but
fish remain off-limits if they have scales but no fins. Those on the
nonkosher list are often scavenging creatures. Cud-chewing livestock with split hooves are considered kosher or clean. Dogs, cats,
and horses are not permitted.

In an era before refrigeration and vaccines, these food laws kept
the Israelites from becoming ill. They also distinguished God's
people. The food prohibitions created social boundaries, ensuring
the Israelites weren't wined and dined by pork-chop-eating pagans
like the Philistines.

Matt explains that these ancient regulations still shape modern food-handling practices. Though the United States Department of Agriculture (USDA) would never claim to base their meat laws on the book of Leviticus, some of the most important rules trace back to the Bible.

"Don't eat sick animals if you don't know what they have—that's USDA," Matt says. "Don't eat dead animals, because you don't know what they died from—that's USDA. Don't eat animals that die of suspicious causes—that's USDA. Even the command to get the blood out—that's USDA."

Table Discovery: The same cut of meat will have different names based on where you are in the United States. According to Matt, a Delmonico is known as the eye of the rib eye on the East Coast but a chuck eye steak in the heartland. A bone-in strip is known as a Kansas City strip west of the Mississippi and a shell steak on the Eastern seaboard.

In addition to food regulations, Jewish teaching also includes laws regarding animal welfare. Ancient Jewish interpreters of the Torah insist one must butcher animals using methods that avoid needless pain. If a blade is nicked, the animal cannot not be consumed. The priestly butcher must constantly inspect the blades to eliminate unnecessary suffering.

Matt quotes King Solomon: "Know well the condition of your flocks, and give attention to your herds." He points out that God has always been insistent about the merciful and humane care of animals. When you give a good life to flocks and herds, they reciprocate in turn by giving life to you and your whole household.

"How we handle animals reflects how we treat others and how we treat God," he declares. "If we are cruel toward animals, we will be cruel to one another."

Today, meat packers have discovered it's in their best interest to consider animal welfare. Temple Grandin, a professor of animal science, revolutionized the industry with new standards for handling, transporting, and processing animals. Matt says big corporations were willing to invest in her methods, because calm, well-handled livestock produce better meat. Whenever an animal is in a fight-or-flight stage, the adrenal glands push excess blood through the body, making it harder to drain and toughening meat. These truths have been embedded in God's Word for millennia.

"Do you feel called to this?" I ask.

"All I want to do is go back to ranching in Oklahoma, but I feel God's saying that's not what I've got for you," Matt explains. "I feel like he's calling me to help people understand where their food is coming from and help people connect through food."

"You really are a Meat Apostle," I affirm.

"People have such flippancy about food," Matt admits. "We're such an abundant country that we don't know where food comes from and we waste 30–40 percent of what we have. People don't get what it takes to raise animals like chickens until they're old or protect a lamb from dying by bottle feeding it day and night."

Matt's eyes turn red and dewy.

"I hurt for farmers and ranchers everywhere. You can't work hard enough on a farm anymore and get ahead. I've seen too many people die an early death from the stress and anxiety of trying to feed others. The American farmer is asked to feed 118 people and can't feed his own family."

Mopping tears with his palms, he adds, "When a farm has been in a family for generations and then gets foreclosed on, it makes me sappy."

HOW TO UNDERSTAND MEAT IN THE ANCIENT WORLD

In the ancient world and in most developing nations today, people view meat as a delicacy because of the intense labor and vast land required to raise the animals. Cows are considered the most valuable because they produce far larger quantities of milk and meat than sheep and goats. They also require more acreage, vegetation, water, and natural resources to sustain. Sheep and goats are often more plentiful because they thrive on smaller tracts of land with limited resources.

Both Abraham's and Job's immense amounts of livestock illustrate their wealth. The psalmist even boasts of the riches of God in terms of animal husbandry as the Lord owns the cattle on a thousand hills. Through modern ears, I'd always heard this as a declaration that God has enough beef for every Outback and LongHorn Steakhouse around.

Those living in an agrarian context understand the declaration in a deeper way. Possessing cattle implies owning the land where the livestock roams. A measure of one thousand hills suggests God's property extends an immeasurable distance, and cattle in the Bible refer to a variety of livestock including sheep and goats.

Their grazing habits complement each other in ideal situations. Cattle go first on the hills and graze the best grasses. Sheep follow behind and clean up the remains. Goats eat what none of the others will. Together they'll graze on a piece of land until it's stripped clean of green. When the land is allowed to rest for a month, the vegetation springs back. God's majesty appears in the creatures, the creation, and the created order.

The vaults of God's wealth run deeper. Unlike our modern culture today, ancient Israelites knew the real value of the animal is found in the length of its life, not its brevity. Cows, goats, and sheep provide an ongoing high-protein source of milk, which can be turned into cheese. Newborns help the flock to multiply. Meanwhile, sheep provide wool for clothing and blankets. In describing God as owning cattle on a thousand hills, the psalmist paints a powerful image of God as Creator and Sustainer and Owner. God has the best and most abundant resources for all generations.

Feeling discouraged? Remember your God owns the cattle on a thousand hills.

Trapped in a scarcity mindset? Be reminded that your God owns the cattle on a thousand hills.

Worried about the future? Rest in knowing your God owns the cattle on a thousand hills.

Livestock are often the centerpieces of powerful biblical stories. To rescue King David from his blindness to adultery and murder, Nathan tells of a wealthy man with an abundance of sheep and cattle.

When an unexpected guest arrives, the rich man refuses to take from his own cattle to prepare the meal. He insists on robbing a poor man of his one ewe lamb. This is the poor man's most prized possession. The fluffy ewe has spent long days following in the man's shadow, lapping from the man's cup, snuggling in the man's arms. Somewhere along the way the animal transitioned from livestock to pet to family member until she became a "daughter to him."

The story stirs the shepherd-king's anger. David loves lambs and knows their value among the poor. If a man had one ewe, then he could convince a neighbor's ram to breed her every year. If a man had one ewe, he had access to milk. If a man had one ewe, he could procure wool to keep him warm. When the rich man slaughtered the ewe, he took more than the man's possession; he took away his future. Through the story, David's eyes open to the error of his abuse of power.

The mention of an animal also appears in the parable of the prodigal son, in which Jesus describes an older brother who becomes embittered when his father celebrates his sibling's return. The older brother's fury centers on the food that's served at the welcome home party. A fattened calf, a true delicacy in antiquity, is butchered and barbecued for the rebellious sibling. But the steadfast brother has never been given even a young goat to celebrate with his friends.

This story would have struck and stuck with listeners whose diet consisted primarily of bread. The peasantry only ate meat during the high holidays, so the idea of butchering an animal for the naughty brother would have caught in their throats.

Jesus highlights the importance of meat again in the parable of the great banquet where a king hosts a marriage feast for his son. The host sends his servants to call those invited, but they refuse. The king can't afford any delay, because the cattle and fatlings have already been killed.

Without access to refrigeration, the host only has a sliver of time before the meat grows rancid. The king sends his servants to the highways and byways to invite any and all. Those who refuse to attend will offend the king and miss the feast of a lifetime. Jesus weaves the story into a cautionary tale warning us not to make the same mistake of refusing the king's invitation.

WHY THE LAMB IS ONE YEAR OLD

All the time talking about meat and antiquity makes me curious to know Matt's perspective on one particular animal: the lamb. At Local Yocal, the largest demand for lamb is always around the Passover.

I am not surprised. In scouring the Bible for mentions of lamb and sheep, one word kept emerging as synonymous with sheep: sacrifice. This traces back to the opening pages of Genesis. Beginning with Adam and Eve, God covers human sin and removes shame with animal skins, marking the first animal sacrifice. Abel, Noah, Abraham, Isaac, and Jacob all made sacrifices which likely involved sheep. God institutes the command to sacrifice as a way to atone for one's sins. Recognizing the high-cost world of livestock helps us understand the high-cost ask of God. Each sacrifice represented an offering of precious resources and future income.

At the Passover, the blood of the sacrificial lamb dribbles down Israelite doorposts and rescues God's people from the knock of death on every door. Later, when the tabernacle appears in the desert, whole burnt offerings, guilt offerings, and sin offerings rise from within its velvety drapes. The first seven chapters of the book of Leviticus describe the main types of animal sacrifice. In burnt offerings, the whole animal is consumed in the fire, an extravagant gift because the entirety is given to God. For guilt and sin offerings, innards are also burned, but the meat is eaten only by the priest. In fellowship or peace offerings, the fat, kidneys, and section of liver burn in the fire. The remaining meat is divided between the priests and the offerer.

Israelite worship could have centered on prayer and piety, but God sets the table in the temple, too. Meat, including lamb, often appears on the altar, filling the holy spaces with savory scents.

The Scripture makes it clear that when making a sacrifice, God prefers his meat roasted instead of boiled.

One of the all-time greatest scenes of sacrifice in the Bible appears during the temple dedication under King Solomon. Twenty-two thousand cattle and 120,000 sheep and goats roast in the mega-meat-tastic event. Some of the offerings are completely consumed, but the rest are enjoyed by the priests and people in a weeklong feast.

As a butcher, Matt describes the scene as impossible to comprehend. The largest, most efficient plants in the nation have the technology and equipment to process 8,000 cattle a day, but that requires 2,200 employees working around the clock. Almost 80,000 family farmers and ranchers are needed to care for six million sheep in the United States—that's one person for every seventy-five sheep.

"What they did is unfathomable—to have that many animals let alone butcher them all," Matt gapes. "All those sacrifices placed the people in a position to trust that God would rescue them, continue to feed them, continue to be their provider."

The Torah gives specific instructions regarding the selection of every lamb that appears on that altar. The animal must be one-year-old and unblemished. Matt explains this detail is deliberate. At one year old, a lamb is mature enough to be full-grown but not old enough to consume more resources than it will return. The yearling represents a year of hard work and investment.

"God wants a person's best," Matt says. "He's saying, 'Don't bring me the lamb you're going to have to kill anyway.' If it only has three legs or lacks an ear, that's not what God wants. He wants our best and to trust him that when we sacrifice, he'll provide the next animal for the offering."

Then the prophet Isaiah promises the long-awaited restoration of God's people will not come through animal sacrifice but human sacrifice. The suffering servant will be a guilt offering for the people of God. Like a lamb led to slaughter before the priests, he will neither resist nor protest.

When Jesus appears on the scene, those who have waited for him don't recognize him. Hoping for a political mover-and-shaker, they forget Isaiah's description of a sheep-like savior, even as John the Baptist cries out, "Look, the Lamb of God, who takes away the sin of the world!"

From a butcher's point of view, it makes sense that Jesus would take on lamb imagery rather than aligning with other livestock.

"A lamb is the most vulnerable animal," Matt explains. "The only thing more vulnerable is a baby chick, because the parents won't defend it."

Those hearing Jesus's words would have understood that John was saying, "Here's the most vulnerable One, or rather the One making himself most vulnerable, who takes away the sins of the world." Perhaps they noticed that John made the declaration near the Passover.

This becomes all the more apparent in the book of Hebrews, where the imagery of sacrificial animal blood reveals the cleansing blood of Christ. For ancient priests, every morning is like the last— standing at the same altar, offering the same sacrifices each day. Christ overturns this system by offering himself as the perfect, unblemished offering, a one-and-done sacrifice for sins.

The scope of Jesus's sacrifice reaches cosmological proportions as God, through Christ, reconciles all things in heaven and on earth to himself, making deep *shalom*, a holy peace, through the blood of God's Lamb.

Then a beloved disciple trapped on the island of Patmos provides a glimpse of this spiritual reality. John's mind-boggling visions in Revelation circle around Jesus as shepherd and lamb. In the New Jerusalem, he says, we will gather around the Lamb enthroned; a place without temple or offering, because he *is* the Temple and Offering.

By the time I leave the Meat Apostle, I know he's given me a lot to chew on—biblically, spiritually, personally, and well, literally. I depart with a deeper appreciation for the life of the animal, its welfare, and the rancher. Matt teaches me to see meat as a treat, as a delicacy, something to savor and enjoy on special occasions.

THE ULTIMATE LAMB

After returning home, I determine to reduce the number of nights a week we eat meat. The transition proves far easier than I expected and makes carnivore-nights extra special. On one such eve, I attempt to grill my first lamb lollipops—petite portions of lamb chops. I breathe in the salty, sweet scent of the sizzling meat. I'm reminded that this is the same aroma that brought God delight in sacrifices.

Table Discovery: Want to begin reducing your meat consumption? Start with meatless Mondays. Get creative making vegetables the star of your meals. I love spaghetti squash pizzas, homemade black bean burgers, and portabella mushroom tacos.

From the Bible's opening to the closing garden scene, sacrifice has always been a part of God's rescue mission. After Noah climbs out of the ark, he serves burnt meats as an offering and the Lord receives them as a "pleasing aroma." God inhales and promises never to flood the earth again. Those scents ascend from the temple whenever the priests sacrifice animals to atone for Israel's sins. With our modern sensibilities, we struggle to wrap our heads and hearts around such activities, but in some beautiful, mysterious way those burnt offerings create a pleasant smell to the nostrils of God. That scent indicates repentance and represents the offer of life, reconciliation with God, and the covering of sin.

Long after Noah arrives ashore, God will ask another father, Abraham, to make a sacrifice, but this time it won't come from among his flock. God tells Abraham to do the unthinkable, to sacrifice his one and only miracle child. The thought makes us scream, "Nooooo! Stop, you crazy old geezer."

Yet the father leads his one and only son on a three-day journey of obedience. As they near the crest of one of the hills in Moriah, Abraham stacks wood on Isaac's back. Atop the mountain, Abraham straps his much-promised and miraculously conceived child to a cross section of lumber.

As Isaac's father reaches toward his son's arteries with the sharpened blade, heaven intervenes with a double shout of Abraham's name. The knife drops to the ground, and Isaac's life is spared. Nearby amid the rustling of a thicket of thorns, a male sheep bleats in distress. Abraham takes the ram and sacrifices it; the scent arises once again to the nostrils of God. Abraham names the place, "The Lord Will Provide."

Sometimes it's hard to fathom how far Abraham was willing to go. Yet this father was ready to offer God the one thing most precious to him. In the nick of time, God rescues Isaac, and in many ways, Abraham too.

A few thousand years later, another sacrifice takes place. A different Father leads his one and only Son on a three-day journey of sacrifice to the same hills of Moriah. Like Isaac, Jesus makes a long, painful journey carrying death on his back. Unlike Isaac, no voice intervenes from heaven and no bushes rustle with the sounds of a scapegoat.

This time the child dies. The Lord provides himself as the sacrifice. Jesus's body hangs from beams, a thicket of thorns punctures his skull, and a sharp blade severs his side. Blood seeps into the soil and darkness descends. The unthinkable has happened and makes us want to lurch forward and yell, "Nooooo! Stop!" as if God were the crazy old geezer.

More than the death of a holy man, this is the massacre of all that is good and true and beautiful. Yet what appears like a lost cause turns out to be a rescue mission. Three days later, Jesus returns to life and flips evil upside down. The once-and-for-all cleansing of sin that is accomplished through Jesus's death and resurrection renders the sacrificial system obsolete. No more goats or sheep or bulls or sons.

Through the bloody mess of Jesus's death, the divine Son knows what it's like to be betrayed by friends, crushed by powers that be, and feel searing pain. The divine Father knows what it's like to watch a son be misunderstood, mocked, and deserted by his friends, and worse, to lose a precious child.

God could have sent his Son in a variety of forms, yet he chose a fragile human body with arteries that bleed, flesh that bruises, and nerve pathways that set the brain afire. In doing so, God experienced what we all experience living on this broken ball of dirt—pain, rejection, betrayal, loss, and grief. As a result, he became the type of God that no other religion claims to believe in: one who can offer his children not just sympathy but empathy. God doesn't say he feels sorry for us but that he knows how we feel. And he really does.

> He became the type of God that no other religion claims to believe in: one who can offer his children not just sympathy but empathy.

When you're crushed by the weight of a child who died before his or her time, God whispers, "I understand."

When you're overwhelmed by chronic pain that befuddles the best doctors, God whispers, "I know how you feel."

When the person you love most fails to come to your defense, God whispers, "I feel your pain."

By becoming flesh and offering himself as a sacrifice for humanity, God crossed the great divide from feeling sorry for our pain to being present in our pain. He became, truly, God *with* us.

This good news gets better. The sacrificial Lamb wasn't content only to feel our pain, he chose to rescue us from the source of our pain—sin. Through his perfect sacrifice, the sting of death is plucked away and the grave no longer has the final say.

The death of Jesus Christ revolutionized history because it ushers in one of the "sweeping historical revolution(s) in the world, namely, the emergence of empathy for victims." With a definitive word, God declared that he would always stand beside and work on behalf of the diseased and dying, the hurting and suffering. And this revolutionizes how we understand the call to be Christlike.

God's ultimate rescue plan is one that he instituted for us and one he wants to institute through us. Just as Christ's sacrifice exhibited both empathy and action, so too Christ calls us to lay down our lives for others in empathy and action. To enter into the pain of others and begin addressing it and alleviating it.

What's the greatest place of pain and trauma for which you've experienced rescue and healing? If you've lost a child, what would it look like to minister to other grieving parents? If you've wrestled with illness or chronic health issues, who is someone you can encourage? If you've felt the pinch of loneliness, rejection, or betrayal, who is an outsider you can include and embrace?

When blood ran down from the Savior to that soil that day, God issued an invitation to all of us: "Do not run from pain, my sheep. Follow the sacrificial Lamb into the dark and trust that he will light the way."

AROUND THE TABLE

Describe a time when you were lost, discouraged, grieving, or in pain, and you experienced rescue and healing. Next, identify one particular situation or struggle in your family, school, workplace, neighborhood, or community that has been on your mind lately. Consider any connections between your pain and your sensitivity to another's pain. Strategize a way to enter into that situation or life and bring the love and presence of Christ.

MARGARET'S LAMB LOLLIPOPS

If you've never prepared lamb before, you'll be surprised by the ease of these delicious lamb lollipops, which provides a bone-in small portioned petite filet.

PREP: 30 minutes   **COOK:** 8–10 minutes   **COOL:** none

8 lollipop lamb chops, ¾ inch thick
2 tablespoons olive oil
1 teaspoon sea salt
¼ teaspoon pepper
2 teaspoons herbes de Provence
2 tablespoons fresh rosemary
fresh juice from one lemon

DIRECTIONS

1. Place the lamb chops on a plate. Drizzle olive oil; sprinkle salt, pepper, herbes de Provence; and squeeze lemon juice on both sides. Let sit at room temp for 20 minutes.
2. Grill the lamb over medium heat (or sear in a hot pan) for 4 minutes. Flip and cook for 3 minutes for medium rare and 6 minutes for medium. Sprinkle fresh rosemary on top and serve.

Serves 2.

SARAH'S BEST PRACTICES FOR A MOUTH-WATERING CHARCUTERIE BOARD

PREP: 15 minutes **COOK:** none **COOL:** none

SHOPPING GUIDELINES:

1. Grab a variety of meats at the deli—salami, pepperoni, prosciutto, or roasted turkey. When choosing the meats and cheeses, ask for samples and buy what looks or tastes yummy. When in doubt, go to Costco and get the packaged meats.
2. Select a variety of cheese flavors (stinky cheeses like blue or mild cheeses like havarti) and textures (soft cheese like brie and harder, aged cheeses like Parmesan). Avoid flavored cheeses (like herb or buffalo).
3. Pick one jam or spread such as fig or whole grain mustard.
4. Include in-season fruit such as apples, figs, grapes, or berries.
5. Select some plain and fun flavored crackers and bread slices like roasted olive and rosemary.
6. Include dried fruits such as apricots to add a burst of color.
7. Sprinkle with a variety of olives and nuts such as Marcona almonds.
8. Garnish with rosemary sprigs (optional).

Serves 4–6.

ORGANIZING THE BOARD:

1. This is an art. Be free and let your creative side take the lead, but also taste different meats, cheeses, and "accessories" (crackers, jams, dried fruit, etc.) together and lay them next to each other, creating beautiful layers and textures and colors. Experiment and remember everything is forgiving and can be moved around. Really. Just start.

2. Meats can't touch each other and need to be on opposite ends or separated by a fruit or nuts. This goes with cheese, too.

3. Lay meat and cheese out first. Along with any bowls (like jam or olives). Then use fruits, dried fruits, and nuts for garnish and fillers. Rosemary and pomegranates can be tucked in places or layered on top of a cheese.

4. Don't forget: Whatever you do, it's going to be delicious. You've got this.

RAY'S MAGICAL MEAT MARINADE

This is a must-have in our household. We use this marinade on steak, chicken, veggies, rice, and more.

PREP: 5 minutes— **COOK:** 4–6 minutes **COOL:** none
plus 2 days to
marinate meat

2 pounds flank or skirt steak
1 cup soy sauce
1 cup sugar
1 cup water
1/2 cup rice wine
1 or 2 tablespoons fresh ginger
3 green onions, chopped
2 garlic cloves, crushed

DIRECTIONS

1. Mix all ingredients in large plastic bag or baking dish.
2. Place meat in marinade for 2 days, turning once or twice.
3. Grill 8–12 minutes and slice across the grain. Happy eating!

Yields marinade for up to 4 pounds of meat.

8

The Perfect Finish

"You can't leave Israel yet," Ido insisted. "You must stay to celebrate Passover with us."

I hesitated. But the adventurer in me couldn't resist a chance to experience the Jewish holiday in the holiest of lands.

On the Friday eve, as the sun sets over the Galilee, I take my seat around a long banquet table. Known as *pesach* in Hebrew, Passover commemorates the freeing of the Israelites from Egyptian slavery. Toward one end of the table rests an oversized plate with six foods representing aspects of the Exodus story.

The shank bone, which still contains a sliver of meat, represents the lamb whose blood on Jewish doorposts saved lives. The shape of the bone is reminiscent of the "outstretched arm" of God, who freed the Jews from slavery.

The brownish egg, which has been boiled and then roasted, symbolizes the offerings that were eaten along with the lamb at Passover during temple times.

The sweet, mahogany balls made from dates and nuts, known as *charoset*, represent the mortar used by the Hebrew slaves to build in Egypt.

Lettuce, soon to be dipped into salt water, alludes to the tears of the Israelite slaves.

A stack of bitter parsley symbolizes the bitterness of slavery.

Matzo wrapped in a special cloth commemorates the Israelites who fled Egypt in such a hurry, they couldn't wait for bread dough to rise.

Extended family members have traveled for the *seder*, the ceremonial dinner, and soon fill the empty seats. Excitement and joy waft through the air. Next to each place setting rests a thin copy of the *Haggadah*, a book used to recount the Israelites' exodus from Egypt. I flip through the pages. Everything is written in Hebrew, which is all Greek to me. I locate an English version on my phone.

Alex, Ido's father-in-law, pours the first of four glasses of kosher wine, and we recite a prayer that acknowledges the holiness of the occasion and offers thanks to the One who created the fruit of the vine.

> "*Baruch atah Adonai, Eloheinu melech ha-olam,*
> *borei p'ree hagafen.*"

> *Blessed are you, Lord, our God, King of the universe,*
> *who creates the fruit of the vine.*

Mama Vered circles the table with a plastic bowl. I watch as others reach into the basin to rinse, then dry their hands with the towel hanging from her arm. Until this moment, I have thought of ritual handwashing with shadowed suspicion.

Long ago, Jesus's disciples forgo the ceremonial handwashing—a slap in the face to the religious establishment. When the religious leaders confront Jesus and ask why he and his disciples break from traditional rituals like handwashing, Jesus responds by asking why they worry about clean hands when theirs are so dirty from impoverishing their parents. It's one of the Bible passages that makes me leery of anything that feels too ritualistic. But in this setting, I discover anew how the rich symbolism of communal practices like these forces us to pause and attune our minds to the divine and one another. This practice reminds us that our hands need cleaning—and our hearts, too.

As I dip my hands in the basin, I catch a glimpse of why Jesus used the opportunity recorded in Matthew's Gospel to double down on the religious rejection of the heart behind the law. The gift of handwashing is much like the gift of the law: it's designed to help us approach others in love and generosity and tender care. I wipe the last droplets from my hands and hang the towel back on Mama Vered's arm. She looks me in the eyes as she says my name in a thick Hebrew accent, and a smile washes over her face. Suddenly, I feel deeply loved.

Next to me sits Jack, a longtime family friend of Ido's who has flown in from London. The family has placed him next to me because he speaks English and can help me understand the evening. Whenever we eat anything, he says, we must lean to the left to symbolize leaving Egypt and breaking free from slavery. Jack reads the perplexed look on my face.

"This is not just about remembering, but also *reenacting* the Passover story," he explains.

I follow Jack's lead and lean to the left to reach a sprig of parsley, later followed by a leaf of lettuce, and I dip them into a bowl of salt water. Even as a salt aficionado, my face curdles from what tastes like seaweed straight from the Gulf of Aqaba. This is the flavor of the pain of God's people.

Alex leads us in another prayer, then cracks a large square of matzo in half to represent the brokenness of slavery. The children watch attentively. They know that one piece of the matzo will become the *afikoman,* the hidden matzo, for them to find. In this household, it's a high stakes game because the child who discovers the treasure can ask for candy, a toy, or money.

Pushing aside the *seder* tray, Alex pours a second cup of wine. Peleg, the youngest of Ido's sons, asks one of the central questions of the night, "Why is this night different from all other nights?"

Alex reads a portion of the *Haggadah,* and the children break out in energetic song, recounting the ten plagues. As they belt out the chorus, our host lifts the plate and walks around the table, tapping the dish on each of our heads twice. I feel like I'm playing a Jewish version of Duck, Duck, Goose, but then Jack explains that the tapping symbolizes how this food-driven story is meant to sink deep into our bones.

Once again, Mama Vered returns with the bowl. Once again, we wash our hands.

Everyone takes a slab of matzo and creates a bitter herb sandwich using the salty greens and flatbread. The flavor curdles my face again, but that is the point: we taste the life of those trapped in slavery.

The table fills with matzo ball soup, gefilte fish, roast chicken, seared lamb, grilled salmon, and—praise Yahweh—steak. *What a celebration,* I think. But I don't realize that the feast has just begun. The first round is followed by brisket, tuna, green beans, almond rice, a fig compote, potato kugel, sweet potatoes, liver pate, and a spiced apple walnut dip.

We eat and eat, and every time I turn around, Grandmother Esther shovels another helping onto my plate. After a week with the family, I've caught onto her wily ways and now, whenever she becomes distracted, I plop more gefilte fish onto her plate. Halfway through the meal, she catches me red-handed and bursts out laughing.

Suddenly my ears sting from the screech of the children's chairs. The hunt for the *afikoman* has begun. A dozen kiddos scatter to scour the house. I try to help clear the dishes, but Mama Vered waves her index finger at me. "Sit, Mar-gar-eet," she instructs as she leans over me. "Do you know why we do this?"

The answer seems obvious, but I feel unsure. "B-b-because it's the Passover?"

"Because they must know where they came from," she announces, gesturing toward the chairs once occupied by the children. "They must know where they came from. This is our story from slavery to freedom."

My eyes follow the pattern of plates and half-eaten dishes, which overflow the table. Together we have been encountering the bitterness of oppression, remembering the hardship of slavery, tasting the salty tears of suffering, sinking our teeth into the bread of affliction, drinking cups of redemption, and retelling a story of deliverance handed down for thousands of years.

The Passover provides a full sensory experience that follows the story of God's liberation of the Israelites. The meal commemorates a physical freedom, but the heart of Passover ushers an invitation for spiritual freedom. To leave behind that which hinders, ensnares, enslaves us. To discover that God satisfies the deepest hungers of our hearts.

The exodus shadows the great salvation to come in Christ. When

Christ came, he fulfilled the story which must also be passed among generations. This is the account of a different Lamb who offered up his body during Passover to free people from the slavery of sin. Just as God asks the Jewish people to commemorate the Passover with a meal, Jesus asks those who hunger for him to commemorate his life with a meal; the same elements that make up the *pesach*—the flatbread and wine—also make up the Eucharist.

Even more radical, Jesus is the meal in the Eucharist. The Bread of Life and True Vine, the two elements, tell us that food will mark our journeys just as it did our Jewish forbearers. Through this commemorative meal, we discover that God wants to satisfy the deepest hungers of our hearts.

The kids tear through every room, emptying shelves and cabinets, searching under boxes and rugs for the hidden matzo. One child shoos the dog in hopes the matzo is under his bed. *Seder* means "order," but we're immersed in chaos right now. Twenty-seven minutes of joyful mayhem later, Peleg returns to the table proudly carrying the matzo once tucked away behind a bookshelf. He wastes no time in making his request—and he soon receives it. He fans out his new stack of cash like a card deck for everyone to see. Peleg is a smart kid, and in a few more years he'll grasp how the *afikoman* symbolizes more than a full piggy bank (kosher, of course), but a type of hunger that leads from brokenness toward healing.

Ido's wife, Yael, appears from the kitchen with a double chocolate ganache cheesecake.

"What is this supposed to symbolize?" I ask Jack with a half-full mouth.

"It's cheesecake, Margaret," Jack chuckles. "It's just dessert."

After a sugary infusion, the children disappear to play outside and the adults stay late into the night exchanging stories and memories. Eight months before my arrival, Ido's father and grandfather passed away within twenty-nine days of each other. This is the first *pesach* without them, and Grandmother Esther has been in a funk all week. I catch sight of tears dripping from the family's eyes between the humorous and honoring stories.

I arrived in Israel a few days before as a stranger, but tonight I am family. I sense the same feeling I had all those years before with my friends Matthew and Ashley and their abundant hospitality. Arriving exhausted yet finding rest and fullness in their loving presence. Tasting fresh food made with loving hands, feasting on the fullness of life—tenderly holding a moment of vulnerability with newfound friends. Even though I am 6,941 miles from the address on my driver's license, I feel like I have come home.

TASTE AND SEE GOD'S GOODNESS

I left Israel after that meal and returned to the United States to begin engaging in a series of expeditions. From fishing to farming, from baking to barbecuing, I experienced God at table after table.

On the shores of Galilee, I learned to live wide-eyed for displays of God's power through fish.

In a fertile valley in California, I discovered the connection between spiritual attentiveness and satisfaction, thanks to figs.

In a seminary kitchen in Connecticut, I found holy community in unleavened bread.

In the darkness of a Utah mine, I uncovered transcendent purpose in glimmering salt crystals.

In a Croatian grove, I encountered divine healing in olive oil.

Around a Texas fire pit, I tasted the desire for God's rescue in lamb.

God is waiting around every table, in every pantry, in every back-yard garden. You just need some fresh ingredients, some time, and a friend or two. No matter where we find ourselves, mealtimes can become sacred spaces of supernatural satisfaction. When we invite God in, he satiates our hunger to know and to be known, to under-stand and to be understood, to love and to be loved. In community, God touches our physical appetites and spiritual affections.

Whenever we gather to eat—whether in a tricked-out kitchen or seated in a borrowed chair with food atop our laps—God is there because all food ultimately comes from him. Yes, God waits in Galilee. But the shores of all our lives are strewn with displays of God's miraculous power. As we break bread, we find the satisfaction of our deepest hungers in the community our souls crave. As we share our lives, we taste and see God's fruitfulness. And when we're tempted to lose heart—and we all will be—we find courage in listening to and participating in the stories of God's rescuing ways. Every table is a doorway, an entrance into a holy and sacred communion with God and those around us.

In the midst of a busy life, we can all create a space to taste and see God's goodness. This begins by recognizing food as a gift from God instead of a commodity. Every mealtime is an opportunity to be on the lookout for Christ to reveal himself in surprising ways. We can all pause in order to pay attention to the One who has pro-vided the food before us.

Food really is God's love made delicious, nutritious, and restorative. But we must learn to slow down and savor the delicate flavors and divine lessons. In a culture rife with consumerism and driven by efficiency, where many meals are handed out a drive-thru window and eaten solo, this isn't the easiest spiritual discipline to practice. But it is well worth it.

May your table be set, not just with food but vulnerability and delight. May your mouth be filled, not just with morsels of meat but with reminders of God's lovingkindness. And may every meal at which you find yourself be a foretaste of the feast to come.

Bon appétit and amen.

Photos

Climbing through shallows of the Sea of Galilee
with local fishermen to catch St. Peter's Fish.

The Sea of Galilee abounds with catfish.

A fig still needing time to ripen.

Looking for ripe figs is like hunting for treasure.

Baking matzo in under eighteen
minutes with Andrew McGowan.

Villa Boscoreale, Italy

Ancient bread similar to
that found in Pompeii.

Our matzo pulled
from the oven.

Drilling equipment inside the Redmond Salt Mine.

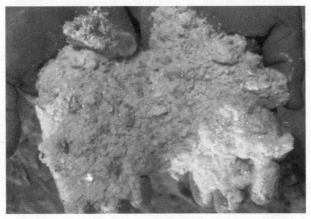

Handfuls of salt from the Redmond Salt Mine.

Olive picking: an afternoon picnic with Natalija and Momma.

Folding the tarp with friends after a long day of olive picking.

Inside the meat cooler with Matt Hamilton
at Steakology 101 class.

Samples of various cuts and types of meat
on the grill at Steakology 101.

The seder plate and overflowing food at Passover
with Ido and his extended family.

Abundant Thanks

Heart books, the ones written from the deepest parts of the soul, are never written in isolation. I've nourished this idea for more than a decade and now I realize that by grace these words were penned in community. This project has been fileted, picked, baked, mined, harvested, butchered, and savored among friends, neighbors, strangers, and loved ones.

Ido, Yael, Esther, Vered, Erez, Peleg, Ella, and Geffen, you took me into your life, your home, your family, your Passover. Your extravagant generosity and abundant kindness brought new life to these weary bones. If you're in Israel, don't miss the opportunity to enjoy Lido (www.lido.co.il).

Yoel Ben Yosef, the curator at Museum of Anchor in Ein Gev, I am grateful for your rich insights into fishing on the Galilee. You let me take home a treasure of yourself and the experience. I will keep them forever.

Carolyn and Richard Hyde, thank you for opening your home and providing a soft landing in Israel when I first arrived. I'm grateful for your rich cultural insights, your generosity, your kindness. To learn more about their work in Israel, visit http://www.heartofg-d.org.

Samuel Smadja, owner of Sar-el Tours and Conferences, who recommended Lido to me. If you ever plan a trip to Israel, reach out to Sar-el Tours at www.sareltours.com.

Thanks to Kevin Herman for introducing me to the joys of figs. Thanks to Andrew McGowan for opening his kitchen and bread recipes; visit his blog at abmcg.blogspot.com. Thanks to Neal Bosshardt of Redmond Salt Mine; visit www.realsalt.com. Thanks to Natalija Hajduk for sharing her olive groves and oil with us. Her husband, Predrag Hedl, is a tour guide, so if you're ever traveling to Stari Grad, you can book him by calling: +385 95 901 3260; email: prezzinjo@yahoo.co.uk; Address: Vatroslava Lisinskog 8, 21460 Stari Grad. Thanks to Matt Hamilton of Local Yocal Farm to Market. The next time you're in McKinney, Texas, (near Dallas) you must visit this amazing store and enjoy a meal; www.localyocalfarmtomarket.com.

Carolyn McCready, Angela Scheff, Tom Dean, Sara Riemersma, Greg Clouse, Beth Murphy, and 52 Watt Studios, ya'll are the dream team. Thank you for your friendship, kindness, and amazingness.

Norman Wirzba, so grateful that you are a groundbreaking leader in the way all of us think about food, God, and the Bible. We're all better because of you.

Jonathan Merritt, without your coaching, cheerleading, and friendship, this book wouldn't exist. You carried me across a finish line for which I didn't have the strength. You breathed life into my weary bones, hope into my weary words, and love into my weary soul. I love you, friend.

James Merritt, you thought I dialed the wrong number after my most difficult day in Israel. Yet you gave me the words I needed to keep going. I'm keeping you on speed dial, buddy.

Carolyn and Alex Garza, sometimes you need an intervention from your besties to know it's time to write again. Y'all and Jon Jon got me back on the field again. Thank you for loving me enough to say the hard things.

Christine Caine, when the Spirit nudged me to ask you for a fisherman on the Galilee, you took up the challenge. In the process, you took this book to a whole new level. Grateful for you.

Jess and Matt Bost, thanks for all the late-night meals and laughter. Who knew your mention of Redmond Salt Mine wound transform our understanding of what it means to be the salt of the earth forever.

Aimee Altizer at Flourish Bakery in Salt Lake City, Utah; Stephanie Krizman of Fleur Bakery in Park City, Utah; and author William Rubel for your rich insights on breadmaking, its history, and ability to transform lives. You are gifts, and your generosity still leave me speechless.

Andrea Townsend, you were my catcher. I threw and threw and threw and you kept throwing more beautiful and cleaner prose back. I love you, friend.

Janella Martinez, oh the times we've had and the places we've been—to think we began with a man named Steve caught in a booby trap. You are one of God's incredible gifts to me.

Tracee Hackel, dear Jesus-loving, theologically grounded, beautiful friend. Thank you for helping me think deeper and more biblically at every turn. So grateful for your catches and edits.

Craig Blomberg, you and Fran still leave me in holy awe. Your humility, your extraordinary love of the scum of the earth, your generosity, your brilliance. Thank you for all your insights, mapping, and catches. But mostly, thanks for being you. God knows we need you.

Leonard Sweet, when I raised the white flag, you were there. Thank you for loving me, loving the church, loving. Kate Bowler, thank you for the phone-a-friend insights. Fred Smith, thank you for your encouragement and insight. Rabbi David Levinsky, thank you for your wisdom and insight. Dave Terpstra, I am so grateful for you, your thinking, your friendship, your healing. Wes and Hannah Stout, thank you for your culinary coaching, recipes, and film suggestions. Liz Curtis Higgs, you gave when you didn't have. Thank you for shattering your alabaster for me, friend. Amy O'Donnell, I'm grateful for your insights and most of all your friendship. Jenni Key, thank you for your copyediting catches. Grateful for you!

Jessica Richie, the depth of your thinking, writing, creativity—well, watch out world for this stunning woman. She's coming for you.

Kari Woodruff, I needed a dietician and nutritionist, and you loved and encouraged and challenged in all your wondrous ways. Thank you, my friend.

Christy and Chris Ferebee, three words: yum, yum, yum. Your recipes are gifts and so are you two. Thank you for making this journey with us. We love you guys.

Leif Oines, love of my life, I promise not to tell anyone I call you Leifington. Oops. I did it again. When I wake up every day the song you sing over me is love. Even. In. This.

Hershey, you snuggled next to me word after word, chapter after chapter, book after book. You are the ultimate trooper.

Recommended Resources

READ

Food and Faith: A Theology of Eating by Norman Wirzba

Eat with Joy: Redeeming God's Gift of Food by Rachel Marie Stone

The Omnivore's Dilemma: A Natural History of Four Meals by Michael Pollan

Not Bread Alone: The Uses of Food in the Old Testament by Nathan MacDonald

Scripture, Culture, and Agriculture by Ellen Davis

The Art of the Commonplace by Wendell Berry

The Supper of the Lamb by Robert Farrar Capon

Intuitive Eating: A Revolutionary Program That Works by Evelyn Tribole and Elyse Resch

Eating Mindfully: How to End Mindless Eating and Enjoy a Balanced Relationship with Food by Susan Albers

Cook's Illustrated Magazine

WATCH

Babette's Feast

Chef's Table

Cooked

Look and See: A Portrait of Wendell Berry

Temple Grandin

Julie and Julia

America's Test Kitchen

Recipe List

DESSERTS

Notes

Chapter 1: An Invitation to a Culinary Adventure

12   "you are understood": As cited online in multiple variations.

18   wild almonds: Numbers 17:8.

18   wilderness of Sin: The Hebrew term "Sin" is unrelated to the English term, though it pops from the text like a droplet of scalding oil. Sin is one of seven wildernesses mentioned with the Israelites' journey from Egypt to Canaan. Scholars estimate that the Israelites arrived at Sin around the time they had likely exhausted all their food supplies and were desperate for food and drink.

18   or as infants: Scientists believe that our desires for particular foods begin in utero during the first trimester as gustatory and olfactory systems develop. Amniotic fluid and breast milk contain molecules from the mother's diet. Foods flavors learned in both the womb and early infancy provide a foundation for food preferences for life. Infants prefer sweet and umami flavors. They reject bitter and sour tastes, perhaps showing a preference for high-calorie, protein-dense foods and an avoidance of potentially toxic or poisonous foods. These preferences can be modified through supportive environment, food availability, and relationships. But research reveals that what we eat growing up—all the way back to the womb—matters. This is interesting in light of the food cravings of the Israelites growing up in Egypt.

19   seventy date palm trees: Exodus 15:27.

21   in for supper: Revelation 3:20.

22   but in our spirits: Thanks to Andrew McGowan for his insightful interview on December 21, 2017. I highly recommend his book, *Ancient Christian Worship: Early Church Practices in Social, Historical, and Theological Perspective* (*Grand Rapids: Baker Academic, 2016*).

22   "the LORD is good": Psalm 34:8.

Chapter 2: A Flaky Filet of Fish

27   bat and bar mitzvahs: A few days after my departure, Ido sent me a picture of the prime minister of Israel enjoying a meal and afternoon speed boat ride with him on the lake.

27   Jewish Renaissance man: The Decks Restaurant (open in summer) and the Pagoda (open year-round) serve scrumptious food. One of my favorites is the steak which is served over Jerusalem pine and olive charcoal. The sushi is fantastic, too. When you visit, look at the legs of the tables, where you'll find that some are marked with a tuna. This is Ido's signature for the pieces he's built.

27   as they do today: A later visit to the original Yigal Allon Museum in Kibbutz Ginosar, where the boat is displayed near its discovery, confirmed that the boat is only 4.3 feet high. The dimensions make the vessel all the more susceptible to the furious storms that whip up waves on the Galilee. Also, I debated for some time whether to use the word *fishers* or *fishermen* in this chapter since women are incredible fishers, too. Leif reminded me that growing up in Alaska, almost all the women he knew preferred to be called "fishermen" over "fisherwomen" or even "fishers," though women's preferences in twenty-first century Alaska probably has little bearing on first century Israel. For an insightful article on this check out: https://parade.com/544561/rachelweingarten/alaskas-female-fishermen-yes-thats-really-a-thing-on-gender-labels-finding-zen-and-weathering-lifes-storms/.

27   it's nearly swamped: Mark 4:37.

28   "Quiet! Be still.": Mark 4:39.

30   bitters the air: Exodus 7:18. Tyler R. Yoder. *Fishers of Fish and Fishers of Men: Fishing Imagery in the Hebrew Bible and the Ancient Near East* (Winona Lake, IN: Eisenbrauns, 2006), 12–19.

31   fresh fish sticks: Numbers 11:5. Supposedly all these "farmed fish" in Egypt gave the people worms, and so the Israelites likely brought a lot of parasites with them out of Egypt. God led them to the bitter waters of Marah where the people drank what one interpreter supposed is lyme-infused water that would have killed all the parasites in their intestines; hence God's promise that they would not suffer from the diseases of the Egyptians (Exodus 15:22–27). Even though the Israelites craved this Egyptian delicacy, it was in fact killing them.

31   don't worship any fish: Deuteronomy 4:16–18.

31   let God's ark go: 1 Samuel 5:1–7.

32   and the Galilee: King Manasseh constructed the gate (2 Chronicles 33:14) and
the sons of Hassenaah rebuilt it (Nehemiah 3:3). The market closed on the Sabbath,
but some Jews tried to circumvent the restriction by purchasing from Phoenician
fisherman. Nehemiah called them out on this. Also, this is the gate through which
Zephaniah predicts that a loud cry will be heard on the Day of the Lord.

32   scales on the skin: https://www.southernliving.com/food/how-to/tips
-how-to-cook-fish.

32   "will be overthrown": Jonah 3:4.

32   heart to his people: Isaiah 50:2; Jeremiah 16:16; Amos 4:2; and
Zephaniah 1:3.

32   meets the Dead Sea: Ezekiel 47:10.

33   God is involved: Living creatures will teem as the purifying power of God
flows like a fountain.

33   good fish from the bad: Matthew 13:48.

33   considered unclean: Leviticus 11:9–10.

35   "for my tax and yours": Matthew 17:24–27.

36   caught with a line: Mendel Nun, *The Sea of Galilee and Its Fishermen in the
New Testament* (Israel: Kibbutz Ein Gev, 1989), 45–46.

37   from the shore: John 21:4–6.

39   sounded enormous to me: You'll find it called the Sea of Tiberias as well as
the Sea or Lake of Ginosar (or Gennesaret). All of these are referring to the same
body of water. The Old Testament uses the name Sea of Kinneret, which means
"harp" because of the harp shape of the lake, in referring to its land allotment of the
twelve tribes of Israel as well as the borders of the Promised Land.

40   "nets for a catch": Luke 5:4.

40   Simon Peter obliges: Luke 5:5.

40   "Leave me to myself.": Luke 5:8 MSG.

41   follow Jesus: Luke 5:11.

41   write them all down: John 21:25.

41   disappointed in their work: Wilhelm H. Wuellner observes, "The first
call is substantively the same as the second call after Easter. Jesus the caller, and
himself the called, together with the disciples, the called and themselves the callers
are the symbol of the New Israel, the community of the called and the calling, the
fished and the fishing, who thus manifest the truth of God as power." Wilhelm H.
Wuellner, *The Meaning of "Fisher of Men"* (Philadelphia: Westminster, 1967), 172.

42 "net was not torn": John 21:11. People have debated the meaning of the 153 fish, but no single theory has won widespread support. The more likely reason, I believe, is simply that it represents just how many fish were actually caught. Then and today fishermen love to count their catches.

43 miracle on miracle: Nun, *The Sea of Galilee and Its Fishermen in the New Testament*, 43. It's worth noting Peter's catch pales in comparison with the two already overloaded boats.

44 strolled with ease: To see and print a copy of a map of Galilee, visit www.margaretfeinberg.com/tasteandsee.

45 God breathed new life: For more details on the cancer journey, read the *Fight Back with Joy* book and Bible study.

45 "fish" in Greek:
I = Jesus
Ch = Christ
Th = God
Y = Son
S = Savior

46 in safe company: https://www.christianitytoday.com/history/2008/august/what-is-origin-of-christian-fish-symbol.html.

Chapter 3: A Plate of Sweet and Succulent Figs

53 every snack between: A frugivore is a fruit eater. If I were trapped on a desert island and forced to survive on a single type of food, I'd pick fruit every time. The vast array of flavors, the kaleidoscope of colors, the rich source of nutrients would make island life more delightful. Plus, I could grow avocadoes, tomatoes, eggplant, okra, and almonds, because those are considered fruit too.

54 cherries for dessert: Fruits in Salt Lake City ripen in a much more condensed time frame because of the short growing season.

54 gleaning unpicked fruit: One of my favorite cherry tree finds is in Sugar House Park in Salt Lake City. If you walk the fenced edges of the park midsummer, you'll discover cherry trees bursting with deliciousness, ripe for the picking, and available to the public.

54 top of my list: "Fruit-forward" is a term often used to describe beverages, including wines and coffees, that are fruity and jammy. Also, I've rarely met a fruit I don't love, except for the durian, which stinks so bad it's illegal on subways in Singapore. I couldn't get past the stench to try it.

54 natural sugars ever since: Genesis 1:1–11.

54   "first fruits": Deuteronomy 26:1–4.

55   technically fruits: Leviticus 25:19, "the land will yield its fruit, and you will eat your fill."

55   means "grape": 1 Kings 18:20 and Joshua 15:50. Even several people are named after fruits. Tamar, the woman who tricks her father-in-law into going on a date with her, means "date" (Genesis 38); Tappuah, a son of Hebron, can be translated "apple" (1 Chronicles 2:43); and Rimmon, the father of Saul's captains, means "pomegranate" (2 Samuel 4:2). For more fruity insights, visit: www.biblicalarchaeology.org/daily/ancient-cultures/daily-life-and-practice/fruit-in-the-bible/.

55   once and for all: Miriam Feinberg Vamosh, *Food at the Time of the Bible* (Nashville: Abingdon, 2004), 42–43. See John 12:13.

55   high priests' robes: Exodus 28:33, 34; 1 Kings 7:20. I've watched YouTube videos on how to eat it neatly, but I prefer ripping open the leathery crimson skin, plucking out the juicy seeds, and popping them in my mouth. But I never eat pomegranates alone. As a messy eater, this is one of those truly messy foods that's best shared.

55   "grapes in the desert": Deuteronomy 24:21 and Hosea 9:10. Jesus also reveals himself as the vine and his father as the vinedresser. It's worth noting a boutique vintner will visit his vines multiple times during a growing season and trim back just a branch, or leaf, or shoot until every cluster yields both maximum flavor and fruitfulness. This imagery reveals God's tender care and intimate involvement with us. In the *Scouting the Divine: My Search for God in Wine, Wool, and Wild Honey* book and Bible study, I spent time with a vintner, shepherd, beekeeper, and farmer in order to better understand the agrarian themes of Scripture. There I explore the vine imagery in depth.

56   fragrance of apples: Song of Songs 7:8.

56   God's instruction: Deuteronomy 32:10; Psalm 17:8; Proverbs 7:2.

56   sin and shame: God replaces the fig leaves with animal skins, also the first animal sacrifice to cover sin and remove shame in the Bible. See Genesis 3:21.

56   Madera, California: Figs, believed to have originated in Mesopotamia, became so beloved among the Greeks and Romans that some even worshiped the fruit. Ancient Olympians were awarded figs for their athletic accomplishments and the Roman author Pliny the Elder celebrated the fruit's healing properties in his writings. In 1796, Franciscan missionaries planted the first fig trees in the United States in Southern California. As their missions advanced up the California coast, the famed Black Mission fig spread throughout the land. From David Sutton, *Figs: A Global History* (London: Reaktion Books, 2014), 8–9. For a

wonderful overview of the history of figs, check out: http://www.bbc.com/earth/story/20170116-the-tree-that-shaped-human-history.

57   I understand why: What's fun about figs is that each variety has totally different flavor aspects. Some are sweeter, savory, or tart, and even textures are different. If you were lucky enough to try a Black Mission first, consider trying other varieties even if you didn't like it. Also check out: https://www.npr.org/templates/story/story.php?storyId=94391625.

57   high perishability: Only increases in customer demand will help change store policies.

58   other fig trees: A few years before, some writers mistakenly assumed all fig trees required caprification, or wasp pollination, to flourish. They described the centers of figs full of insect carcasses from wasps who sought sweet nectar and died inside. Fig sales dropped as a result of the false reporting. Calimyrna figs (which require wasp pollination) declined from half the figs grown in California to less than 500 acres. "What they failed to mention," Kevin told me, "is the fig tree is a cousin of the rubber tree. The sap is so caustic it would dissolve the remains of wasps if there were any. It's the same reason my workers have to be covered head to toe."

58   "early fruit on the fig tree": Hosea 9:10.

59   the more one discovers: Sutton. *Figs: A Global History*, 18.

59   learns of Jesus: John 1:44–51.

59   Jesus and his love: Luke 19:1–9.

59   sun-dried and processed: All the shaking reminds me of the words of the prophet Nahum: "All thy strong hold shall be like fig trees with the first-ripe figs: if they be shaken, they shall even fall into the mouth of the eater" (Nahum 3:12 KJV).

60   it will be cut down: Luke 13:6–9.

61   "summer is near": Matthew 24:32.

62   everything else: Insights drawn from Barbara Brown Taylor, *Bread of Angels* (Lanham, MD: Cowley Publications, 1997), 156–158.

62   different person: Daniel J. Simons and Daniel T. Levin, "Change Blindness: Theory and Consequences," *Psychonomic Bulletin & Review*, 1998, 644–49.

63   shape our perceptions: https://www.verywellmind.com/what-is-change-blindness-2795010.

63   "fruit from you again": Mark 11:14.

64   their own fig tree: See, for instance, Micah 4:4.

64   fig tree has withered: I asked Kevin if it's possible for a fig tree to wither that fast. There's a virus called the fig leaf mosaic virus, he says. It doesn't kill the whole tree, but he's gone out on a Sunday and the tree is fine; on Tuesday, it withers; by Friday, the branches appear dead. Whether or not the virus was involved, the Gospel account grounds us in Christ's authority over creation.

64   "fruit from you again": Mark 11:14.

65   work of the Holy Spirit: Galatians 5:22.

66   "simply, and unaffectedly": Oswald Chambers, *My Utmost For His Highest* (Grand Rapids: Discovery House, 1992), May 18.

Chapter 4: A Loaf of Bread Just Out of the Oven

77   unleavened bread: In arguing over the duration of how long after water hits flour it will begin to leaven, the rabbis decided to base it on the length of time that it takes to walk a "mil" (a Talmudic unit of distance). Because they loved the law of God and thought nothing as important as keeping it, the rabbis believed that the best way to help people observe the law and keep them from even getting close to violating it either intentionally or unintentionally was to put up a "fence" around the law (this phrase is based on Deuteronomy 22:8, in which the people are commanded to build fences around the roofs of their houses to keep people from falling off and thus making the homeowners guilty of manslaughter). The "fence" consisted of rabbinic guidelines that, if observed by the people, would keep them far away from breaking the law of God because the "fence" requirement exceeded the basic requirement of the law. If there were any dispute between two guidelines, the stricter was always considered the better. In this case, twenty-four minutes to bake bread would keep you from violating the law against leavening, but if twenty-four minutes is good, eighteen is better because it is six minutes further away from violating the law. One wonders if these rabbis may have regretted their decision to place the "fence" so far out when they got home and explained the new requirement to their wives, who had to bake the bread.

78   the most conservative burn it: As in other kosher eateries, Ido's waitstaff work for weeks before Passover as well as all night before the festival, scrubbing every inch of the restaurant and then redesigning the menu as leaven-free for the upcoming week.

78   Pharisees and Sadducees: Matthew 16:6 NASB. Various translations use the word "yeast" instead of "leaven" throughout the Bible.

79   also known as *farro:* Exodus 9:32, Isaiah 28:25, and Ezekiel 4:9all use "spelt" in the NIV translation.

80   "but commemorative": Today, nonorthodox Jews have developed creative culinary ways to make matzo delicious during the week of Passover, including homemade chocolate toffee matzo, nine-layer no-bake matzo cake, and s'mores.

82   Nom, nom: Goat butter is a great option for those with dairy allergies who enjoy the tangy taste. Also, the phrase "nom nom" is thought to have originated with the sounds made by Cookie Monster when eating cookies.

82   Genesis 4:20; Genesis 4:22. Researchers debate whether the original harvested grains sprouted in the Fertile Crescent regions of Africa or in the Middle East. When humans shifted from hunter-gathering to domestication, they planted grains. At first, those hard kernels proved difficult to chew and hard to digest, but if the exterior was removed and the broken grains were mixed with water, a porridge emerged. One day, whether by accident or culinary experiment we'll never know, flour and water were seared by heat, and the first loaf was baked.

82   invention of the plow: In later days, the prophets would proclaim peace by describing swords beaten into plowshares (Isaiah 2:4; Micah 4:3), but the plow allowed people to grow grain more efficiently and effectively.

82   received as a gift: The end product looked much different from the refined flour we enjoy today. With thick, uneven flour marred by stones, teeth were often shattered and broken from the bread in the ancient world, archaeologists have discovered.

82   Arab Spring uprisings: Some identify social media as the instigator of the Arab protests. While it played a significant role, the protests were preceded by a series of bad grain years and a sudden rise in the cost of the grains. See: https://www.npr.org/2011/02/18/133852810/the-impact-of-rising-food-prices-on-arab-unrest and https://www.motherjones.com/politics/2011/07/climate-change-food-crisis-price-bread-political-instability and https://www.pbs.org/newshour/world/world-july-dec11-food_09–07.

83   gluten intolerance: http://www.uchospitals.edu/pdf/uch_007937.pdf and https://www.forbes.com/sites/rosspomeroy/2014/05/06/are-you-really-gluten-intolerant-maybe-not/#441e399e2a20.

83   low-carb lifestyle: Skipping bread has become an American fad alongside a much-needed diet alternative for those with food allergies and other medical conditions. I was surprised that many gluten-free breads and desserts are higher in calories and more fattening than those with gluten.

83   "have food to eat": Genesis 3:19 NASB and NIV.

83   person to walk: Leviticus 26:26 KJV.

83   "millet and spelt": Ezekiel 4:9.

84   nightmarish news: Genesis 40:15–17.

84   baby is on the way: Genesis 18:6.

84   bread of ravens: Genesis 25:34 and 1 Kings 17:6.

84   you guessed it—bread: Judges 7:13; Ruth 2:14.

85   delicious provision: Exodus 9:18 CSB; 16:4.

85   "[presence] of the LORD": Exodus 16:6–7.

87   "among so many": John 6:9.

87   food of peasants: John 6:9, 15.

87   "broken pieces": Matthew 14:20.

89   "this is my body": John 6:35; Matthew 6.11; Matthew 26:26.

92   "will live forever": John 6:51.

Chapter 5: A Dash of Sea Salt

103   cease to beat: "Take It with a Grain of Salt," *Harvard Heart Letter*, November 2006. Salt consumption around the world varies widely. A teaspoon of salt contains 2,300 mg of sodium. According to Harvard research, the Yanomamo people of the Amazon rainforest live on just 200 mg of sodium a day, the average American consumes 3,400 mg a day, and those in northern Japan consume 26,000 mg of salt each day.

103   salt-producing empires: Mark Kurlansky, *Salt: A World History* (New York: Penguin, 2002), 38.

104   the word "salary": https://www.seasalt.com/history-of-salt. By the Middle Ages, those who sat near the host were "above the salt" and those seated further away were "below the salt."

104   sustain its troops: Multiple battles were fought over Saltville, Virginia. During the Second Battle of Saltville on December 20–21, 1864, the Union army succeeded in destroying the saltworks and cutting off salt access to the Confederates.

104   poor of India: Staff article, "A Brief History of Salt, *Time Magazine*, March 15, 1982.

105   human consumption: The Great Salt Lake is a geological wonder worthy of your next visit to Utah. Antelope Island State Park offers a visitor center, and

Bridge Bay has a swimming beach. The summer gets wildly hot, so be prepared. The water allows you to float without effort. But you'll definitely want to pack some good soap and a towel for a shower afterward. And while you're packing, make sure your car is full of fuel, and take some cool beverages and snacks. For a fascinating look at how the Great Salt Lake differs from the Dead Sea, listen to: https://www.npr.org/2013/04/26/179224937/great-salt-lake-is-no-dead-sea.

106   from the mine: Neal went to great lengths to secure permission for the tour since the public isn't allowed in the mines.

108   ego once dwelled: "Awe, the Small Self, and Prosocial Behavior," Paul Piff, Pia Dietze, Matthew Feinberg, Daniel Stancato, and Dacher Keltner, *Journal of Personality and Social Psychology*, published online May 18, 2015.

108   sweet flavor: Himalayan salt, the closest comparison to Redmond salt, has only become popular in the United States over the last two decades. Neal hopes consumers will realize the benefits of salt mined with their natural minerals.

109   in our kitchen: Neal shared that if you ever find yourself in a pickle over salt or you're simply using salt to make pickles, simply call 1–800-FOR-SALT for advice. You can find an incredible array of Redmond Salt Mine products under the Real Salt label.

109   sodium chloride: Genesis 19:26.

109   "no one lives": Jeremiah 17:6.

109   water is no more: 2 Kings 2:21; Judges 9:45. And who can forget a fellow salt aficionado, Job, who asks, "Can that which is tasteless be eaten without salt?" to describe the depths of his grief (Job 6:6 ESV).

109   new way forward: The tossing of salt on the land is also a war technique to prevent the growth of future food as well as delineate from the past.

110   growth of bacteria: Ezekiel 16:4. This practice is not recommended today because too much salt can injure an infant.

110   and sodium too: Exodus 30:34–35.

110   call to worship: Leviticus 2:13.

110   woody aromas: Sara Kinonen, "8 Salt-Infused Fragrances That Will Inspire a Beach Getaway," *Allure*, May 18, 2017.

110   "before the LORD": Numbers 18:19 ESV.

111   "salt of the earth": Matthew 5:13.

112   "trampled underfoot": Matthew 5:13.

112   as an influencer: If you're cooking and the lid falls off your shaker, you can overpower the strong salinity in different ways. Adding an acid like fresh

lemon juice or vinegar will lessen the influence of salt by adding a strong, new flavor. If you've dumped excess salt on a slab of meat, place the meat in water and the water will overcome the salt by leeching it out of the meat. If you've just added a little extra salt, consider adding a potato which will also reduce saltiness.

113   "it is thrown out": Luke 14:34–35.

113   need it too: One surprising discovery is that following 21st-century tsunamis that struck several countries in Southeast Asia, some farmers experienced bumper crops after the seawater receded. "Tsunami boosts rice yields, agriculture in Aceh province," Associated Press, September 26, 2005. https://news.mongabay.com/2005/09/tsunami-boosts-rice-yields-agriculture-in-aceh-province/.

113   fresh, new life: Anthony B. Bradley, *Christianity Today*, September 23, 2016.

113   the word "salvation": A Latin speaker in the first century might have thought of this, but it's worth noting that in the Greek, Hebrew, and Aramaic, the words for "salt" and"salvation" bear no relationship to each other.

114   of the earth: The Talmud, meaning "study" or "learning," is a collection of writings that cover Jewish law, tradition, and custom. This work was compiled between the third and sixth centuries AD.

Chapter 6: A Bowl of Delectable Olives

122   community flabbergasted: 2 Kings 4.

123   down for the season: Historically, farmers left the olives on the higher branches until Easter as one of the few foods that carried families through the long winters.

124   "previous generations": Proverbs 22:28 NLT.

124   to become tasty: Some people will eat dried olives straight from the tree.

125   slate-gray the next: Mort Rosenblum, *Olives: The Life and Lore of a Noble Fruit* (New York: North Point, 1996), 195.

126   "drive you mad": Rosenblum, *Olives*, 7–18.

127   steeped in oil: Oblicas are some of the most common olives harvested in Croatia.

129   his deep peace, too: Genesis 8:6–12. God extends the olive branch and communicates his promise to save and heal those who are at war with him. God reconciles himself to humanity and humanity to one another. In Noah he establishes his people, specifically through his son Shem, and also brings peace

between humanity and creation as the waters subside and they thrive in the newly washed earth. All point to God's ultimate peace bought in Christ's sacrifice and established in his return.

129   into the manna: Numbers 11:8.

129   pomegranates and olive groves: Deuteronomy 8:8.

130   "in fruit and form": Jeremiah 11:16 NASB.

130   strong olive trees: Psalm 52:8.

130   the trees' roots: Psalm 128:3.

130   "pure olive oil": Hosea 14:6 and Psalm 128:3.

130   from slavery to freedom: Exodus 25:8, 31–40; Exodus 27:20. One of the most stunning and detailed descriptions of an ancient oil lamp came from the golden luminary with seven branches that were ever lit in the second temple of Jerusalem.

130   healing to the land: Exodus 29:7.

130   liquid gold: 1 Samuel 10:1; 1 Samuel 16:13.

130   supply of oil: 1 Chronicles 27:28.

130   wave offerings: Leviticus 14:21, 24.

130   overlaid with gold: 1 Kings 8:7.

130   olivewood into the doors: 1 Kings 6:31–32.

130   one in abundance: Isaiah 11:1–2. Jesse is the father of David, and Jesus is born from the line of David.

132   olive oil as their base: Esther 2:12.

133   more than skin deep: Psalm 92:10; 45:7; 104:15.

133   pain reliever ibuprofen: "Olive Leaf," *Alternative Medicine Review*, March 2009, 62–65.

133   antioxidant properties: Barbara Barbaro, Gabriele Toietta, Roberta Maggio, Mario Arciello, Mirko Tarocchi, Andrea Galli, and Clara Balsano, "Effects of the Olive-Derived Polyphenol Oleuropein on Human Health," *International Journal of Molecular Science*, October 2014, 15(10): 18508–24.

133   "pretty good health": Jane Fonda, *Prime Time* (New York: Random House, 2011), 137.

133   "olive heals, you know": Though it never appears in Scripture, one of the lesser-known healing properties of olive oil is its use as a laxative. In some countries today, like Trinidad and Lithuania, you'll find bottles of olive oil in drugstores right next to Ex-Lax.

134   taste like cigarettes: Oil is so perceptive that if shipped aboard a vessel with petroleum, users will taste the gasoline.

134   vulnerable and fragile: J. E. Holoubek, A. B. Holoubek, "Blood, Sweat and Fear: A Classification of Hematidrosis," *Journal of Medicine*, 27 (3–4): 115–33.

135   Jesus petitions: Luke 22:42.

135   they slather are healed: Mark 6:13.

135   our ailments, as well: Some scholars note that the Hebrew word for oil, *meshha*, points to the relationship between the three persons of the Trinity as expressed using the terms Anointer, *mashoha*; Anointed, *mshiha*; and Anointment, *meshha*. That suggests God is the Anointer, Christ is the Anointed One, and the Spirit is the Anointment. See Dudley Martin and Geoffrey Rowell, eds., *The Oil of Gladness: Anointing in the Christian Tradition* (Collegeville, MN: Liturgical Press, 1993), 26–33.

135   oil and pray: James 5:14.

139   *you are my praise. Amen.*: The first part of the prayer is the Jewish blessing said before eating fruit, and the second part of the prayer is Jeremiah 17:14.

Chapter 7: A Flame-Grilled Lamb Chop

144   prone to more illness: http://www.nytimes.com/2002/03/31/magazine/power-steer.html.

146   horses are not permitted: Leviticus 11.

146   pagans like the Philistines: The area where the Philistines lived is famed for its pork production. Even today, you could go and eat at an orthodox Jewish friend's house, but they could not come and eat at yours.

147   "that's USDA": See Leviticus 11:1–8. The Bible affirms that "the life is in the blood" (Leviticus 17:11). So removing the blood shows a respect for the life God created and acknowledges God's created order. Not eating food with blood is the one food restriction that is placed on Noah and his descendants (Genesis 9:3–24) and one of the only two food restrictions that the infant church kept intact (Acts 15:29), at least when ministering to the Jews.

147   unnecessary suffering: https://pdfs.semanticscholar.org/1946/b833f1c6b19e4ea3891c809dc18c9b7d3df4.pdf.

147   "attention to your herds": Proverbs 27:23 (ESV), 24–27.

147   "cruel to one another": Randall Lockwood and Frank R. Ascione, *Cruelty to Animals and Interpersonal Violence* (West Lafayette, IN: Purdue University Press, 1998). This incredible volume provides startling correlations between animal

cruelty and human cruelty. Thank you to the American Humane Society for raising awareness of this important issue.

148   processing animals: I highly recommend the film about her life titled, *Temple Grandin*.

148   toughening meat: "Sometimes people say their steak is bloody, but that is just water and platelets," Matt explained. "If an animal is butchered and the blood isn't drained, then it coagulates in the flesh. Blood is jelly, and few people want to eat gelatinous meat." It's worth noting that draining the blood removes blood-related diseases.

149   illustrate their wealth: Genesis 12:16; Job 1:3.

149   a thousand hills: Psalm 50:10.

150   "daughter to him": 2 Samuel 12:2–4.

151   celebrate with his friends: Luke 15:23–29.

151   already been killed: Luke 14:15–24.

152   first animal sacrifice: Genesis 3:21.

152   likely involved sheep: Genesis 4:2–4; 8:20; 13:18; 26:25; 33:20; 35:7.

152   priests and the offerer: Leviticus 1–7. https://www.bibleodyssey.org/en/passages/related-articles/sacrifice-in-ancient-israel.

153   weeklong feast: 2 Chronicles 7:4–10.

153   seventy-five sheep: Some scholars point to the perfectly round numbers and suggest these figures represent Jewish hyperbole. The numbers in the lamb industry today are found at www.americanlamb.com/lamb-101/american-lamb -industry/.

153   one-year-old and unblemished: Numbers 29:36.

153   neither resist nor protest: Isaiah 53:7.

154   "sin of the world": John 1:29 ESV.

154   near the Passover: John 2:13. Jesus leans into this vulnerability motif when he compares sending his disciples out like a flock of lambs into a wolf pack. Also see Luke 10:3.

154   cleansing blood of Christ: Hebrews 9:13–14.

154   God's Lamb: Leland Ryken, *Dictionary of Biblical Imagery* (Downers Grove, IL: InterVarsity Press, 1998), 56.

154   Temple and Offering: Revelation 7:17; 14:1–4; 21:22–23.

155   "pleasing aroma": Genesis 7:23; 8:21.

155   flood the earth again: Genesis 9:11.

156   "The Lord Will Provide": Genesis 22:1–14.

156   old geezer: Idea for this sparked and adapted from Barbara Brown Taylor, *Gospel Medicine* (Lanham, MD: Cowley Publications, 1995), 60–62.

158   "empathy for victims": Philip Yancey, "Why I Can Feel Your Pain," *Christianity Today*, February 8, 1999.

158   alleviating it: Hebrews 4:14–5:10; 9:23–10:25.

Chapter 8: The Perfect Finish

165   Egyptian slavery: The customs used to celebrate the Passover were under Sephardi rules; Ashkenazi has different customs.

165   shank bone: The shank bone commemorates the Passover sacrifice offered at the temple in Jerusalem before the Romans destroyed it in AD 70.

165   Jews from slavery: Psalm 136:12.

165   during temple times: The egg, like the other foods, has multiple interpretations. It also symbolizes the triumph of life over death.

167   impoverishing their own parents: Matthew 15:1–6.

170   chocolate ganache cheesecake: The cheesecake, a nondairy recipe as Jews are not allowed to have milk after meat, was one of the most incredible I've ever eaten.

Free
Gifts

I am so delighted that we have the opportunity to Taste and See God's goodness together. In appreciation and celebration, I've put together some free gifts for you— including fun party invitations, posters, recipe cards, and bonus recipes. I'd love to send these to you for your surprise and delight. Simply email us at:

hello@margaretfeinberg.com

New Video Study for Your Church or Small Group

If you've enjoyed this book, now you can go deeper with the companion video Bible study!

In this six-session study, Margaret Feinberg helps you apply the principles in *Taste and See* to your life. The study guide includes video notes, group discussion questions, and personal study and reflection materials for in-between sessions.

Study Guide
9780310087816

DVD
9780310087847

Available now at your favorite bookstore, or streaming video on StudyGateway.com.

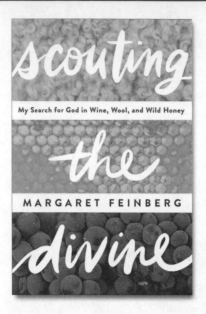

A HUNGRY CHILD
CAN'T LEARN AND GROW

*Together you and I can make sure children
become all God created them to be!*

Sponsor a child today and receive a free copy
of Margaret Feinberg's *Taste and See*

compassion.com/tasteandsee

margaretfeinberg.com

Savor Life. Nourish Friendships. Embark on New Adventures.
at www.margaretfeinberg.com

On the site, you'll find:

- Weekly giveaways
- Free e-newsletter sign-up
- Margaret's personal blog
- Interactive discussion board

- Video and audio clips
- Secret sales and promotions
- Travel schedule
- Great prices on Bible studies

 become a fan on facebook
facebook.com/margaretfeinberg

 become a twitter
follower
@mafeinberg

 become an instagram
follower
@mafeinberg